Contents

SIMPLY PERFECT
PARTY CAKES
for kids

Easy Step-By-Step Novelty
Cakes for Children's Parties

Introduction

It has been a dream of mine to write a book dedicated purely to kids' party cakes, I have children and I know how special it can be to choose and create the right centrepiece for their all-important birthday parties and events. I wanted to step away from the typical Disney and commercial routes to create designs that are guaranteed to make the children smile and will be remembered for years to come.

Within this book I share some fresh ideas that cater for children of every age group: from an adorable tiered baby's first birthday cake to a bright and bold paintball-themed design for older teenagers. You will find ideas to suit a wide variety of personalities and interests, with perfect cakes for fairy tale princesses, budding superheroes, disco divas, surfing dudes, trendy 'tweens' and many, many more. I will also give inspiration on how to adapt the cakes and tailor the designs to suit boys or girls where possible.

I believe that making party cakes should be as stress-free and enjoyable as the party itself and have provided a range of projects – some very easy and others a little more challenging. However, with easy-to-follow instructions accompanied by clear step-by-step photography, handy tips, technique guidance and a range of templates to use, each project will be easily achievable, even for beginners.

A variety of modern techniques have been included throughout the book, including silver leafing, stamping, using edible icing sheets and creating designs inside the cakes to really surprise your guests. If you are running short of time to make the main designs or want to include a little extra treat for the party tea or to give as favours, each project includes a variation design for cookies, mini cakes or cupcakes that are sure to delight.

I hope that you will be inspired to use the techniques as you like, and that you will enjoy making showstopping party cakes that are as unique and fun as the children themselves!

Zoe
x

Tools and Equipment

The following checklists contain the essential equipment you will need for baking the cakes in this book, plus any handy tools for creative work. It is useful to organize these and have them to hand before you start baking. Any specific tools that are required in addition to the basics are listed in the You Will Need lists within the individual projects.

Baking Essentials

- **Electric mixer** for making cakes, buttercream and royal icing
- **Kitchen scales** for weighing out ingredients
- **Measuring spoons** for measuring small quantities
- **Mixing bowls** for mixing ingredients
- **Spatulas** for mixing and gently folding cake mixes
- **Cake tins** for baking cakes
- **Cupcake or muffin trays (pans)** for baking cupcakes
- **Baking tray (sheet)** for baking cookies
- **Wire racks** for cooling cakes

GENERAL EQUIPMENT

- **Greaseproof (wax) paper or baking (parchment) paper** for lining tins and to use under icing during preparation
- **Cling film (plastic wrap)** for covering icing to prevent drying out and for wrapping cookie dough
- **Large non-stick board** to put icing on when rolling it out (alternatively you may roll out icing on a workbench using a dusting of icing sugar to prevent sticking)
- **Non-slip mat** to put under the board to prevent it from slipping on the work surface
- **Pastry brush** for brushing sugar syrup and apricot masking spread or strained jam (jelly) onto cakes
- **Large and small sharp knife or scalpel** for cutting and shaping icing
- **Large and small serrated knives** for carving and sculpting cakes

- **Cake leveller** for cutting even, level layers of sponge
- **Large and small palette knife** for applying buttercream and ganache
- **Icing or marzipan spacers** to give a guide to the thickness of icing and marzipan when rolling out
- **Icing smoothers** for smoothing icing
- **Spirit level** for checking that cakes are level when stacking them

- **Kitchen towel/tissue**
- **Metal ruler** for measuring different heights and lengths
- **Plastic sleeves** for storing icing when not in use to prevent it from drying out
- **Cake scraper** to scrape and smooth buttercream, ganache or royal icing, used in a similar way to a palette knife

Creative Tools and Materials

- **Large and small non-stick rolling pins** for rolling out icing and marzipan
- **Hollow plastic dowels** for assembling cakes
- **Turntable** for layering cakes
- **Double-sided tape** to attach ribbon around cakes and boards
- **Piping (pastry) bags,** paper or plastic, for royal icing decorations and piping swirls on cupcakes
- **Piping tubes (tips)** for royal icing decorations
- **Cocktail sticks (toothpicks) or cel sticks** for holding sugarpaste details in place
- **Edible glue** for sticking icing to icing
- **Edible pens** for marking details on sugarpaste
- **Cake-top marking template** for finding/ marking the centre of cakes and marking where dowels should be placed
- **Fine paintbrushes** for gluing and painting
- **Soft brushes** for brushing edible dust onto icing
- **Ball tool** for frilling or thinning the edge of flower (petal/gum) paste
- **Circle cutters** for cutting circles of various sizes
- **Shaped cutters** for cutting out shapes such as flowers, ovals and hearts for icing and cookies
- **Clear alcohol** for mixing into dust to paint on icing and for sticking icing to marzipan
- **Trex (white vegetable fat)** for greasing the board, pins and moulds

Baby Buttons and Bunting

This adorable cake was inspired by a piece of gift-wrap. The addition of sugar buttons and stitched details, together with colourful bunting and cute elephants and birds, makes it the perfect design to celebrate a christening or new baby. The grey background colour is neutral, but you could tailor it for a girl or boy by omitting the flowers or changing the colour scheme.

You Will Need

MATERIALS

- 10cm (4in) round, 10cm (4in) deep; 15cm (6in) round, 11cm (4¼in) deep; and 20cm (8in) square, 11cm (4¼in) deep cakes (see Cake Recipes), each iced in grey sugarpaste (rolled fondant) (see Covering with Sugarpaste)

- 28cm (11in) square cake drum covered with grey sugarpaste at least 24 hours in advance (see Icing Cake Boards)

- 45–60ml (3–4 tbsp) royal icing (see Royal Icing)

- Flower (petal/gum) paste: 30g (1⅛oz) white, 80g (2⅞oz) dusky blue (mix blue and black), 65g (2⅜oz) dusky baby pink (mix pink and brown), 50g (1¾oz) dusky deeper pink (mix a larger quantity of pink and brown), 50g (1¾oz) mustard (mix yellow and ivory), 50g (1¾oz) aubergine (mix purple, pink and brown), 40g (1½oz) olive green (mix green and brown), 15g (½oz) dark grey

EQUIPMENT

- Six hollow pieces of dowel cut to size (see Assembling Tiered Cakes)

- Grey grosgrain satin ribbon: 1.75m (2yd) length of 1cm (⅜in) wide, 1.15m (1¼yd) length of 1.5cm (⅝in) wide

- 1cm (⅜in) circle cutter

- Templates: large elephant, bird, bunting triangles (see Templates)

- Stitching tool

- Six petal blossom cutter: 3.3cm (1⅜in)

- Five petal blossom cutters: 2.6cm (1in), 2.2cm (⅞in)

- Cutting wheel

- Button moulds (FPC and Squire's Kitchen moulds)

1 Dowel and assemble the cake tiers onto the iced cake drum, using three dowels in the bottom tier and three in the middle tier. Secure the tiers in place with royal icing. Wrap 1cm (⅜in) ribbon around the base of each tier, securing it in place with double-sided tape (see Securing Ribbon Around Cakes and Boards).

2 Very thinly roll out the white flower paste and use the circle cutter to cut out enough circles to cover the cake in a polka dot fashion. Using a small amount of edible glue, space the dots evenly, starting with the bottom tier and keeping the same distance horizontally between the dots as vertically. I tend not to measure the distance between the dots, but if you find it difficult, use a ruler.

3 The dots on the upper tiers are started at the back of the cake. On the 15cm (6in) tier, place one dot at the bottom then two above: one in the middle of the tier and one at the top. Go around the cake in one direction, spacing the dots evenly, with roughly the same distance between the dots horizontally as vertically. Fill the gaps in-between with more dots. The top tier is slightly shallower, so miss out the top row of dots, but try to keep the spacing consistent.

4 Roll out about 40g (1½oz) of dusky blue flower paste to approximately 1mm (¹⁄₁₆in) thick. Use the templates provided (see Templates) to carefully cut out the elephant and two triangular pieces with a scalpel or sharp knife. Run the stitching tool all the way around the outside of the shapes and set the triangles aside under a plastic sleeve to prevent them from drying out.

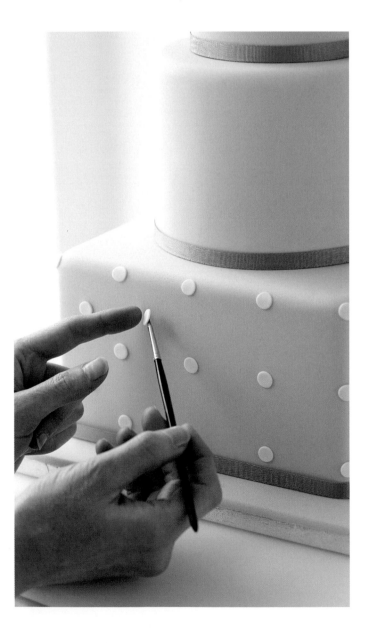

5 Place the elephant up against the right side of the front of the cake. Before you stick it in place, remove all the dots that would be hidden behind it, including those that would only be partly covered. They should come off easily if you haven't used too much glue, however you can use a sharp knife if necessary. Now use edible glue to attach the elephant in place.

6 Cut out fresh white dots from the remaining white flower paste. Trim them to fit around the elephant, keeping to your polka dot pattern, and attach using edible glue.

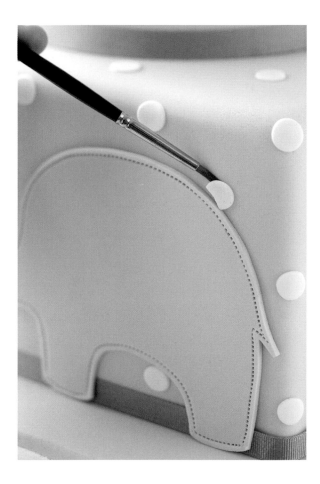

7 Roll out just over half of the dusky baby pink flower paste to 1mm (1/16in) thick and cut out the elephant's ear, the bird and two triangles using the templates provided (see Templates). Run the stitching tool around each shape. Stick the ear onto the elephant using edible glue. Attach the bird on the top tier, removing any dots that would sit behind it first and replacing them with freshly trimmed dots (see Step 5). Set the two triangular pieces of dusky baby pink flower paste aside with the blue ones under the plastic sleeve.

8 Roll out the dusky deeper pink flower paste to 1mm (1/16in) thick and cut out two more triangles and the bird's wing using the template (see Templates). Run the stitching tool around the edge of each shape, stick the wing onto the bird with edible glue and place the triangles under the plastic sleeve with the others.

9 Repeat to cut out two more triangles each from the mustard and aubergine flower paste and mark them with the stitching tool. Mark a faint point at the top of the middle tier in line with the right corner of the square tier. Mark another point on the opposite side of the middle tier in line with the back left corner. Visualize a curved hanging line between the two points on each side of the cake. There is no need to mark this, as the placing does not need to be exact.

10 To make the bunting on the middle tier, attach one of each coloured triangles onto the front left side in a curve. Remove any white dots first and replace them with trimmed ones (see Step 5) once the triangles are in place. Make sure that the triangles are fairly evenly spaced, approximately 5–10mm (1/4–3/8in) apart. Stick the remaining six triangles around the back of the cake to match the front.

11 Roll out the remaining coloured flower paste fairly thinly and cut out different sized blossoms using the three blossom cutters. Use edible glue to secure between two and four blossoms on each side around the bottom tier, making sure they are evenly spaced apart and positioned low down on the tier. Continue to remove and replace the white dots as you go (see Step 5). Stick about nine or ten more blossoms around the top two tiers, among the bunting and the bird.

12 Roll out the olive green flower paste to 1mm (1/16in) thick. Use the stitching tool to mark straight lines along the length of the paste, keeping each line close to the next. You will need enough stems for each flower around the bottom tier. Make straight cuts at either side of the stitching lines using a sharp knife. Stick the stems around the cake with edible glue, trimming them to fit under the flower heads as you go.

13 Use a cutting wheel or a sharp knife to cut out small leaves in slightly different sizes from the remaining olive green flower paste. Run the stitching tool through the centre of each leaf, from the tip to the base. Randomly stick one or two leaves onto the flower stems and coming out from underneath the 'floating' blossoms, trimming them at the base using the matching blossom cutter if necessary.

14 To make the buttons, lightly smear some Trex (white vegetable fat) into the button mould. Roll a small ball of coloured flower paste to fill the mould. Push it into the mould and smooth the back flat with your fingers. Pop the button out of the mould, trying not to distort the shape. Make a button for the centre of each flower, varying the size and colour, and secure in place with edible glue.

> ─ TIP ─
>
> If you find that the button isn't coming out of the mould easily, put it into the freezer for five minutes to firm up before removing it.

> ─ TIP ─
>
> When making the buttons you may need to test the size of the mould first with a piece of paste, then re-roll into a ball to ensure a smooth, crease-free finish.

15 Thinly roll out the dark grey flower paste and cut tiny 10 x 1.5mm (⅜ x ¹⁄₁₆in) strips for the bunting string. Use edible glue to secure the strips between and overlapping the triangular pieces to join up the bunting. Cut another tiny strip for the elephant's eye and stick it to the elephant in a curve. Cut three more tiny pieces and attach to the eye to create stitched eyelashes. Lastly, roll a tiny ball for the bird's eye and attach it in place using edible glue.

16 Secure a length of 1.5cm (⅝in) grey grosgrain satin ribbon around the base drum (see Securing Ribbon Around Cakes and Boards).

Extra Inspiration

Use the flowers and birds to decorate simple cupcakes (see Baking Cupcakes) in silver cases (liners), covered in grey sugarpaste (see Covering Cupcakes with Sugarpaste) with the same polka dot design.

Cute Elephant Cookies

These beautiful bespoke cookies are cut out using the elephant template from the Baby Buttons and Bunting cake. Adding flower paste details to the royal iced cookies is a great way of using the stitching tool and flower button decorations to perfectly complement the main cake.

You'll Also Need

- Cookies (see Baking Cookies) cut out using elephant templates: there are two sizes provided to make smaller and larger cookies (see Templates)

- Royal icing (see Royal Icing)

- Food paste colours to match the dusky blue, dusky pink and grey in Baby Buttons and Bunting

- Coloured flower (petal/gum) paste to match the colours in Baby Buttons and Bunting

- Two or three sugar blossoms with button centres and leaves (see Steps 11–14, Baby Buttons and Bunting)

- Stitching tool

- Cutting wheel

1 Outline and flood the cookies (see Royal-Iced Cookies) with blue, pink or grey royal icing.

2 For the ear, thinly roll out coloured flower paste and use the elephant's ear template (see Templates) to cut out the shape. Run the stitching tool around the edge and attach it on to the cookie with edible glue.

3 Make the eyes (see Step 15, Baby Buttons and Bunting) and secure them on to the elephant, along with the flowers and leaves using edible glue.

Teddy Bears' Picnic

This classic design is perfect for baby's first birthday or a little girl's tea party. Modelling sugar bears is a handy technique to have in your repertoire, as the basic body parts can easily be altered to form other animals. The picnic basket, with its weave texture, miniature modelled food and cute tea set, completes the cheerful scene.

You Will Need

MATERIALS

- 18cm (7in) square, 11.5cm (4½in) deep cake (see Cake Recipes), freshly iced in beige (mix ivory and brown) sugarpaste (rolled fondant) (see Covering with Sugarpaste)

- 150g (5½oz) beige sugarpaste to match cake icing mixed with 0.75ml (⅛ tsp) CMC (Tylose) (see Modelling Paste and CMC)

- Flower (petal/gum) paste: 200g (7oz) white, 40g (1½oz) pale blue, 5g (⅛oz) brown, 50g (1¾oz) pink, 5g (⅛oz) darker pink, 5g (⅛oz) green

- 400g (14oz) coffee-coloured modelling paste (mix brown and white)

- Quarter quantity of royal icing (see Royal Icing)

- 30cm (12in) round cake drum iced with ivory sugarpaste (see Icing Cake Boards)

EQUIPMENT

- 11cm (4¼in) basket weave embosser patchwork cutter

- 5mm (¼in) strip cutter (No. 2 Jem)

- Circle cutters: 1cm (⅜in), 1.5cm (⅝in); 2cm (¾in), 2.5cm (1in), 3.5cm (1⅜in)

- Piece of spaghetti

- Ribbon: 2m (2¼yd) length of 1.5cm (⅝in) beige, 1.25m (1⅜yd) length of 1.5cm (⅝in) blue

1 Press the basket weave embosser into the sugarpaste covering, starting on one side and working all the way around the base of the cake. Next go around the upper part of the cake. The design won't meet perfectly as the cutter isn't tall enough, however any overlap will be covered later by the satin band and bow.

─ TIP ─────────────

Do not press too hard in the centre with the basket weave embosser, as the texture will poke through the picnic blanket, making it look bumpy.

3 Roll out a quarter of the beige sugarpaste into a thin sausage about 75cm (29in) in length, first using your hands, then using a smoother to make the roll even. Fold it in two then start twisting the sugarpaste strands to create a rope-like effect. Repeat this three more times using the rest of the beige sugarpaste.

2 Press the design into the top of the cake in the same way, smoothing it out if necessary. Pay attention to the corners, which will be visible.

4 Brush some edible glue around the top edge of the cake. Stick one piece of rope onto the front of the cake, trimming each end halfway along the sides. Stick the next piece around the back top edge and trim again halfway along each side, joining up with the first piece. Repeat with the last two pieces around the bottom of the cake.

5 To make the picnic blanket, roll out 150g (5½oz) of white flower paste to 3mm (⅛in) thick and cover under a piece of plastic. Roll out the pale blue flower paste to 2mm (1/16in) thick and use the strip cutter to cut out stripes. Remove the plastic on the white flower paste and lay the stripes on top, spacing them out evenly. Carefully press the stripes into the paste, rolling the paste to 2mm (1/16in) thick. Cut a 20cm (8in) square and attach the blanket onto the cake with a small amount of edible glue.

7 To make the smaller bear's legs, roll 16g (½oz) of coffee-coloured modelling paste per leg into a ball and then form the balls into rough cone shapes. Use your finger to taper the narrow parts, leaving wide feet. Use a knife to trim the ends, cutting diagonally down and away from the feet. Repeat the process for the larger teddy bear using 18g (⅝oz) of modelling paste per leg. Attach the legs onto the bodies with edible glue.

8 To make the arms, use 10g (¼oz) of coffee-coloured modelling paste per arm for the smaller bear and 12g (⅜oz) per arm for the larger bear. Roll the paste into a sausage shape then taper it into a point. Attach the arms onto the bears using edible glue. The girl teddy has an arm resting on a foot and the boy has both arms coming around in front of him.

6 To make the smaller bear's body, roll 90g (3¼oz) of the coffee-coloured modelling paste into a ball and then form it into a cone shape. Repeat for the larger bear, this time using 95g (3⅜oz) of modelling paste. Stick a piece of spaghetti down through the centre of each bear and snap it off about 2.5cm (1in) above the top of the body.

> **TIP**
>
> Use additional glue on the tops of the teddy bear's feet to help to secure the arms in the correct position.

9 Roll 40g (1½oz) of modelling paste into a ball for the smaller bear's head and 45g (1⅜oz) for the larger bear's head. Mix a pea-sized amount of the coffee-coloured modelling paste with the same amount of white flower paste. Split the paste into two, roll two more balls and squash them flat. Stick one onto each of the bears' faces with edible glue and use the edge of a 1cm (⅜in) circle cutter to mark on their smiles. Secure the heads on top of the bodies, pushing them over the spaghetti.

10 Roll two tiny pieces of brown flower paste for the bears' noses and draw in the eyes with black edible pen. For the ears, roll two pea-sized amounts of beige sugarpaste for each bear, indent the centres with the end of a paintbrush or ball tool and attach them to the bears' heads using edible glue. Leave to dry.

11 For the smaller bear's bow, thinly roll out 35g (1¼oz) of pink flower paste to approximately 10cm (4in) long and 4cm (1½in) wide. Cut even 0.75–1cm (½–⅜in) wide strips along the length of the paste. Take one strip and wrap it around the bear's neck, securing it in place with edible glue and cutting to size if necessary.

12 Take another pink flower paste strip, trim it to 8cm (3¼in) long, and then pinch it in the middle and at each end. Fold and glue the two ends into the middle to form the loops. Use the 2cm (¾in) piece cut from the loop strip to make the knot. Fold over the sides first and wrap and stick it around the centre of the loops. Pinch one end of two remaining strips to form the bow's tails. Stick the tails to one side of paste around the bear's neck, with one overlapping the other, then attach the bow on top with edible glue. Trim the tails with scissors.

13 To make the modelled cake, thinly roll out the leftover pink flower paste and cut out four discs with the 2.5cm (1in) circle cutter. Roll out about 20g (¾oz) of white flower paste and cut out three discs of the same size and one disc using the 3.5cm (1⅜in) circle cutter for the plate. Stick the discs together with edible glue, as shown, then roll nine tiny balls from the darker pink flower paste and attach in place.

14 To make the teapot, roll 10g (¼oz) of white flower paste into a ball then into a bulb shape, flattening the top and bottom. Mark the top with the 1cm (⅜in) circle cutter. Cut out a 1.5cm (⅝in) circle for the base and indent around the edge with the end of a paintbrush. Roll a tiny sausage for the handle, cut another 1.5cm (⅝in) circle for the lid and roll a tiny ball to go on top. Stick the teapot together with edible glue.

15 To make the cupcake held by the smaller bear, roll a tiny tapered cylinder from pink flower paste and use a sharp knife to indent ridges all the way around it. Roll a tiny thin sausage of white flower paste and coil it around to make the buttercream swirl. Top with a small ball of darker pink flower paste and stick the cupcake together with edible glue.

16 To make the sandwiches, simply cut small squares of green flower paste, sandwich them with white flower paste then cut them into triangles. Make a round plate from white flower paste using the 2cm (¾in) circle cutter, attach one sandwich triangle using edible glue and stick this to the larger bear's paws. Make another plate with the 2.5cm (1in) circle cutter and attach the sandwiches onto this with edible glue.

17 Make the teacup from a small, wide cylinder of white flower paste topped with a disc of brown flower paste. Roll a thin sausage of white flower paste for the handle and attach in place with edible glue. Cut out a round disc plate from white flower paste using the 1.5cm (⅝in) circle cutter and attach the teacup to this using a small amount of edible glue.

18 Secure the bears onto the cake with some royal icing. Stick the picnic items onto the cake using edible glue if they are still slightly wet, or royal icing if they are dry.

19 Wrap the beige ribbon around the cake to cover the join in the basket weave. Secure in place at the front and back with double-sided tape. Make a little bow and stick it onto the ribbon with more double-sided tape. Finish by securing the blue ribbon around the base drum (see Attaching Ribbon Around Cakes and Boards).

Sweet Treat Cookies

Children will adore these cute cookies, designed to look like their favourite cakes and buns. With their matching pastel colour scheme and clever piping, they are the perfect treat for any picnic or party and you can make the designs as simple or as intricate as you like.

You'll Also Need

- Plain edged or fluted cookies (see Baking Cookies): 2.5cm (1in), 5cm (2in) and 6.5cm (1½in) round, 5cm (2in) square

- Small–medium-sized piping (pastry) bags filled with very soft-peak royal icing (see Royal Icing) in white, pink and brown for the cake toppings and fillings

- Four small piping bags with no. 1 tube (tip) filled with soft-peak royal icing in baby blue, white, pink and darker pink

- Two medium piping bags filled with flooding icing in baby blue and white

- 2cm (¾in) sausage piece of white flower paste for the candle

LAYERED CAKE COOKIE

1 Outline and flood the large, round cookie with baby blue royal icing (see Royal-Iced Cookies) to make the plate. Set aside to dry then pipe on the tiny dots with soft-peak baby blue royal icing (see Piping with Royal Icing).

2 Use very soft-peak pink royal icing to pipe a wiggly line around and slightly over the top edge of three 5cm (2in) cookies for the iced layers, then fill in the cookies. Allow to dry, then stack and stick the cookies onto the iced plate cookie, as shown, using royal icing. Pipe tiny balls of darker pink icing around the edge of the cake.

3 Pipe a small blob of soft-peak white icing in the centre to secure the candle, then pipe a dot on top of the candle and pull it upwards to form the wick.

ICED BUN COOKIES

1 Outline and flood the square cookies with white icing to make the plates. When dry, pipe a scallop border around the edge for additional decorative detail. Stick it on top of a smaller cookie so it is lifted up slightly, almost like a pedestal.

2 To make the buns use white and brown very soft-peak royal icing to ice the top of half of the 2.5cm (1in) cookies in the same way as for the pink icing on the layered cake. When dry, stick them on top of their bases with a good amount of filling so it oozes out of the side a little. Decorate the tops with pale pink swirls and darker pink balls using the soft-peak icing.

3 Attach as many buns as desired in place on the cookies using more royal icing.

Treasured Toy Chest

This traditional toy chest cake, complete with its realistic woodgrain effect and cute collection of nursery favourites, is a simple yet delightful design to make for a first birthday celebration. The toys are so easy to model – many originating from a basic ball shape – and you can have fun altering the design to add the recipient's favourite playthings!

You Will Need

MATERIALS

- 20 x 12.5cm (8 x 5in), 10cm (4in) deep rectangular cake (see Cake Recipes) on a base board (5mm (¼in) foam board or cake card), thinly iced using the panelling method (see Covering with Sugarpaste)

- Sugarpaste (rolled fondant): 1kg (2lb 4oz) ivory/caramel-coloured, 1.5kg (3lb 5oz) chocolate-coloured mixed with 15ml (3 tsp) CMC (Tylose)

- Modelling paste: 340g (11¾oz) beige (mix ivory and brown paste food colouring), 100g (3½oz) pink (see Modelling Paste and CMC)

- Flower (petal/gum) paste: 5g (⅛oz) black, 5g (⅛oz) brown, 150g (5½oz) white, 100g (3½oz) pale blue, 25g (1oz) red, 20g (¾oz) orange, 20g (¾oz) yellow, 80g (2⅞oz) green, 65g (2⅜oz) purple

- Quarter quantity of royal icing (see Royal Icing)

EQUIPMENT

- 33cm (13in) cake drum

- Metal ruler with flat end

- Stitching tool

- Piece of spaghetti

- Cutters: 6cm (2½in) star, 1cm (⅜in) circle, letters

- 110cm (44in) length of 1.5cm (⅝in) pink gingham ribbon

1 Cover the cake drum with ivory/caramel-coloured sugarpaste (see Icing Cake Boards). Press the length of a metal ruler across the sugarpaste at regular intervals to make six indentations. Next use the flat end of the ruler to make perpendicular indents at intervals across the board so that the markings resemble floor boards. Set the cake drum aside to dry for at least 8–12 hours.

2 To make the planks of wood covering the toy chest, start by measuring the height and width of each end of the cake. Divide the height by three to get the width measurement for the three planks on each end. Roll out a large piece of chocolate-coloured sugarpaste to 5mm (¼in) thick and cut out six planks of wood, each measuring approximately 13 x 3.75cm (5 x 1½in). Use the pointed end of a stitching tool to mark indentations to resemble the grains on each piece.

3 Starting at the base, secure the planks to each end of the cake using a small amount of edible glue. Use the ruler to slightly separate the planks and ensure they sit neatly on the cake.

TIP

When baking the toy chest cake, I start with a 18cm (7in) square cake, cut about 4cm (1½in) off from one side and move it round to one end of the cake to make it rectangular. The cake can then be trimmed to the correct size.

4 Measure the width across the front of the box to get the length of the planks for the front and back of the toy chest: it should be approximately 22cm (8½in). The width will be the same as for the end pieces: approximately 3.75cm (1½in). Roll out some more sugarpaste, cut out six larger planks and use the stitching tool to mark the grains on the wood (see Step 2). Stick them onto the front and back of the cake with edible glue.

TIP

The rabbit can be made in advance of the cake. You could even make a couple of rabbits and keep one back to decorate another project.

5 For the planks on top of the toy chest, measure the width of the top, add on 5mm (¼in) to create a lip and divide by three: it should be approximately 5cm (2in). The length will be the same as for the front and back: approximately 22cm (8½in). Cut the planks out, indent the grains as before, and secure the planks in place using edible glue.

6 To make the rabbit, first knead 135g (4¾oz) of the beige modelling paste for the body. Roll into a smooth crease-free ball, before tapering one end into a slight cone shape. If the modelling paste feels too soft and is unable to hold its shape, add a small amount of CMC (Tylose) (see Modelling Paste and CMC). Insert a piece of spaghetti into the body to support the head then run the stitching tool down the front, back and two sides.

7 Each leg is made from 35g (1¼oz) of beige modelling paste. Roll each leg into a sausage shape, then taper the ends and squash them flat slightly. Run the stitching tool around each leg and secure onto the rabbit using edible glue, tucking the tapered ends underneath the body a little. Repeat for the arms, using 30g (1oz) of beige modelling paste for each one. Taper one end of each arm into a point before attaching them to the shoulders with edible glue.

8 For the rabbit's head, knead about 35g (1¼oz) of beige modelling paste well and roll it into a smooth ball before forming it into an egg shape. Set the head aside on your work surface to harden slightly – you may need to reshape it a little as it starts to dry and hold its own shape. Run the stitching tool down the front and sides of the head. When dry, secure the rabbit's head onto the spaghetti on the body with edible glue, making sure the spaghetti does not pierce through the top of the head.

9 Make two 20g (¾oz) tapered sausages from beige modelling paste for the ears, squash them flat slightly at one end and run the stitching tool around the sides. Stick them onto the rabbit's head using edible glue. Finally roll two tiny black flower paste balls for the eyes, and form a small triangular piece and two tiny strips from brown flower paste for the nose and mouth. Secure the features onto the rabbit's face with edible glue.

10 To make the book, roll out about 80g (2⅞oz) of white flower paste to 2mm (1/16in) thick and cut out three pages, each measuring 7.5 x 8.5cm (3 x 3⅜in). You may need to reroll the paste to cut out all three. Roll out the pale blue flower paste to 2mm (1/16in) thick and cut out a 9 x 8cm (3½ x 3¼in) rectangular piece for the book sleeve. Fold the book sleeve in half to sandwich the white book pages in-between, securing the pages with a small amount of edible glue if necessary. Thinly roll out a marble-sized piece of yellow flower paste, use the cutter to make the star shape, and finally attach it onto the front of the book jacket with a little edible glue.

11 To make the coloured ring stacker, roll 70g (2½oz) of white flower paste into a ball, squash it flat slightly, then use an icing smoother to square off the sides a little. For the rings, roll balls from the following flower paste colours: 25g (1oz) red, 20g (¾oz) orange, 15g (½oz) yellow and 10g (¼oz) green. You will need to cut out a hole from the green piece using the 1cm (⅜in) circle cutter. Flatten each ring slightly then stack them up, one on top of each other, in the order shown. Secure the rings in place using edible glue. Roll a pea-sized piece of yellow flower paste into a short sausage and insert it into centre of the green ring to form the top of the stacker.

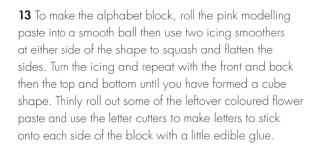

12 To make the toy ball, roll a 60g (2¼oz) ball of green flower paste and a 60g (2¼oz) ball of purple flower paste. Cut them in half and then into quarters. Take two quarters from each colour, arrange them so the matching colours are opposite each other and secure together using edible glue. Roll a tiny piece of white flower paste to cover the join at the top of the ball.

13 To make the alphabet block, roll the pink modelling paste into a smooth ball then use two icing smoothers at either side of the shape to squash and flatten the sides. Turn the icing and repeat with the front and back then the top and bottom until you have formed a cube shape. Thinly roll out some of the leftover coloured flower paste and use the letter cutters to make letters to stick onto each side of the block with a little edible glue.

14 Attach the alphabet block onto the iced board with a small amount of royal icing. Assemble the toys on and around the cake using royal icing if the toys are dry, or edible glue if they are wet.

TIP

Use the leftover quarters of green and purple flower paste to make a second ball, if desired. You could even alter the design to feature a whole host of toys spilling from an open toy chest!

15 Finish by securing the pink gingham ribbon around the base board (see Attaching Ribbon Around Cakes and Boards).

Rubber Ducky Mini Cake

I fondly remember my son playing with his rubber duck in the bath when he was a baby. It always made me smile to see the enjoyment he got from splashing it about in the bubbles and seeing it pop up again, so I was happy to recreate one from modelling paste on this cute block mini cake.

You'll Also Need

- 7.5cm (3in) deep, square mini cake, made from two layers of cake (see Mini Cakes), iced in blue sugarpaste (rolled fondant) (see Covering with Sugarpaste)

- Flower (petal/gum) paste: white, orange, black

- 4cm (1½in) star cutter

- Yellow modelling paste (see Modelling Paste and CMC)

- Royal icing (see Royal Icing)

- Small piece of spaghetti

1 Thinly roll out the white flower paste and use the cutter to make four stars; one for each side of the block. Attach the stars to the cake with a small amount of edible glue.

2 Roll a large ball of yellow modelling paste for the duck's body. Taper the end into a point and carefully tease it upwards to form the tail. Insert the spaghetti where the head will be placed. Roll two modelling paste balls for the wings. Shape them into elongated cones, flatten them into petal shapes then use the end of a paintbrush or the back of a knife to make indents at the point on each wing. Attach them in place with edible glue.

3 For the duck's head, roll a smaller ball of yellow modelling paste, push it onto the spaghetti and secure with edible glue. Roll some orange flower paste into a ball for the beak top and form a cone before flattening the tip slightly. Tilt the end upwards and secure it in place. Roll another small orange flower paste cone, flatten it again and attach it to the bottom of the beak. For the eyes, roll two very small black flower paste balls, flatten them and attach them in place with edible glue. Roll two tiny white flower paste balls, flatten them and stick them on top of the eyes. Secure the duck onto the cake using royal icing.

TIP

You may need to adjust the shape of the beak slightly once it is in position using the end of a paintbrush or the back of a small knife.

Round and Round the Garden

This cute garden scene with its pretty quilled flowers and butterflies will really appeal to little girls, although you could easily tailor it for boys by replacing some of the flowers with spiders, worms and beetles! I love the quilling technique – simple to create with a strip cutter and so different to the classic appliqué usually seen in cake designs.

You Will Need

MATERIALS

- 12.5cm (5in) round, 11.5cm (4½in) deep cake and 20cm (8in) round, 12.5cm (5in) deep cake (see Cake Recipes) with Chequered Circles effect (optional) (see Inside Cakes), both iced in white sugarpaste (rolled fondant) (see Covering Cakes with Sugarpaste)

- One 28cm (11in) round cake drum iced in foliage green sugarpaste (Sugarflair) at least 24 hours in advance (see Icing Cake Boards)

- Flower (petal/gum) paste: 400g (14oz) white, 20g (¾oz) black

- Paste food colouring: violet (Wilton), claret, red extra, peach, baby blue, grape violet, egg yellow, gooseberry, Christmas green, foliage green (Sugarflair)

- Quarter quantity of royal icing (see Royal Icing)

EQUIPMENT

- 5mm (¼in) strip cutter (No. 2 Jem)

- Small piping (pastry) bag

- 90cm (35½in) length of 1.5cm (⅝in) green ribbon

1 Start by mixing up the coloured sugarpaste (see Colouring Icing). You will need between 20–40g (¾–1½oz) of sugarpaste for each colour: 20g (¾oz) for the smaller shapes and 40g (1½oz) for the larger flowers and main flower stems. Once coloured, keep the sugarpaste in plastic bags to prevent it from drying out.

If you want your cake to look the same as mine, use the following paste food colouring:

- **Pink flower:** claret for the petals and a stronger claret for the centre.

- **Red flower:** red extra for the petals and mix peach with a touch of red extra for the centre.

- **Blue flower:** baby blue for the petals and mix baby blue and grape violet for the centre.

- **Large butterfly:** claret for the body and mix claret and violet for the wings.

- **Small butterfly:** peach for the wings and egg yellow with a touch of white flower paste for the body.

- **Ladybird:** red extra for the body and black flower paste for the head.

- **Caterpillar:** gooseberry.

- **Bees:** egg yellow for the body and a small amount of white flower paste for the wings.

- **Quilled flower stems and leaves:** Christmas green.

- **Swirly fronds and frilled stems:** foliage green.

- **Frilled flower:** violet for the frilled petals and mix violet and a touch of claret for the centre.

TIP

I have used a large variety of colours, however you could easily simplify the colour scheme to save time colouring if you prefer.

---

2 The majority of the shapes in this project begin with a basic 'coil'. To make a basic coil shape, thinly roll out the flower paste and use the 5mm (¼in) strip cutter to cut out 18cm (7in) pieces of an even width.

3 Take a strip and curl one end around a cocktail stick (toothpick), then continue wrapping the strip around it until you reach the end. Place the coil down on the work surface. You can keep it tight or loosen it by using the cocktail stick to tease the paste outwards. The size of the coil will depend upon its tightness and the length of the paste strip used.

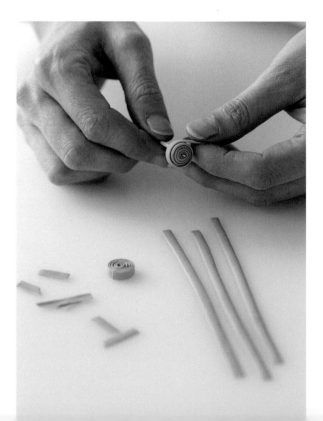

4 For each pink flower, you will need to make five tight coils from 12cm (4¾in) long strips of claret-coloured flower paste for the petals and a 10cm (4in) long strip from the darker claret flower paste for the centre. When making the coils, ensure that the end of the strip is positioned towards the centre of the flower, the stem or the inside of a shape for a neat finish. The design is repeated at the back of the cake, so you will need enough coils to make two pink flowers. Set the flowers aside and cover with a plastic sleeve if necessary. You can leave them to dry out a little, although ideally, you will need to keep the underside slightly wet.

5 The red flowers are slightly larger, so you will need to make six coils from 15cm (6in) strips of red extra-coloured flower paste for the petals. Loosen the coil a little using a cocktail stick before pinching the point at the end of the coil to form a 'teardrop' shape. Make a small simple coil for the centre from an 8cm (3¼in) length of the peach/red mix paste. This will be attached on top of the petals when they are assembled on the cake. Repeat to make a second red flower.

6 For the blue flower, you will need to make five coils from 15cm (6in) lengths of baby blue-coloured flower paste for the petals. Pinch the edge of each coil into a point for the edges of the petals. Make the centre by cutting a 0.7 x 7cm (⅜ x 2¾in) strip of blue/violet mix flower paste by hand and make it into a coil as before. Set the coil aside – this will be attached inside the outer petals when it is assembled onto the cake later. Repeat to make a second blue flower.

7 Make the small and large butterflies, ladybird, caterpillar and bees using the same basic coil and teardrop formations, referring to the main photograph and colour guide in Step 1 for guidance. Simply change the length of the strips to adjust the sizes of your designs – for smaller shapes use shorter coil lengths and for larger shapes use longer coil lengths.

8 Make the leaves in same way, using 17cm (6¾in) strips of Christmas green-coloured flower paste formed into coils. This time pinch both sides of the coil to form the basic leaf shape.

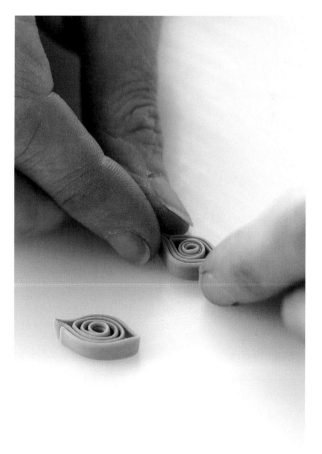

9 To make the fringed flower, cut out a 1.5cm (⅝in) wide strip of thinly rolled out violet-coloured flower paste by hand for the petals. Trim it to approximately 10cm (4in) long and using a scalpel or sharp knife, cut slits all the way along the strip, about 1–2mm (¹⁄₁₆in) apart and three quarters of the way into the width of the paste. For the centre, use the strip cutter to cut a 7cm (2¾in) long strip from violet/claret mix flower paste and glue to one end of the fringed piece. Coil the flower as before, starting with the thin strip for the centre of the flower. Brush a little glue along the bottom edge of the fringed paste and continue to roll the flower up all the way to the end, so that the fringe is wrapped around the centre three times. Trim the end if necessary and carefully open out the individual petals using a cocktail stick. Set aside to dry.

10 Make the flower stems by forming strips of foliage green or Christmas green-coloured sugarpaste, either leaving them straight or curling them slightly at the ends. Make the smaller fronds and antennae in the same way, using shorter strips of paste in your desired colours.

11 Allow everything to dry slightly. When the stems are stiff enough to hold their own shape, apply edible glue to one side and stick them in place on the cake. This can be fiddly – hold the stems in place for a few seconds to ensure they are secure and be careful not to smudge glue over the cake. Space the flowers out and trim the stems to create varying lengths. Stick the fronds and leaves onto the stems with edible glue to give them extra support.

12 Once all the stems are in place, starting sticking the flowers to the cake using edible glue. If you are worried that the glue will not hold them, use a tiny amount of royal icing, especially for the fringed flower. Next, glue all the bugs and butterflies in place in the same way.

13 To make the grass, roll out the Christmas green-coloured flower paste and cut out 1.25cm (½in) wide fringed strips. Secure the strips to the cake in-between the stems, trimming them to size as you go. Use the end of a paintbrush or a cocktail stick to help you tease some of the blades forward for a three-dimensional effect.

14 Fill a small piping bag with some royal icing and fill in the gap between the bottom tier and top tier if there is one visible. Use a small, damp paintbrush to smooth the icing neatly around the base of the top tier.

15 Finish by securing some green ribbon around the base board (see Securing Ribbon Around Cakes and Boards).

Extra Inspiration

Use the same techniques to decorate mini cakes (see Mini Cakes) with cute flowers, bugs and butterflies for perfect garden party treats!

Garden Gang Cookies

These gorgeous cookies, with swirly piped lines mimicking the quilled effect on the main cake, are perfect for an summer picnic or tea party. I used cutters to make the butterfly, ladybird and flower and designed a template for the bee. Use your imagination to create your own designs to add to your garden gang!

You'll Also Need

- Vanilla cookies (see Baking Cookies), cut into butterfly, ladybird and flower shapes with cutters; bee shape cut from template (see Templates)

- Royal icing (see Royal Icing)

- Paste food colouring: red, black, yellow, claret, purple

- Small and large piping (pastry) bags

- No. 1 piping tubes (tips)

1 Start by colouring the royal icing (see Colouring Icing). You will need two piping bags of each colour: a small piping bag for outlining and a large piping bag for flooding, both using no. 1 piping tubes.

LADYBIRD
Outline the wings with red-coloured royal icing, then outline the head and the gap between the wings with black royal icing (see Royal-Iced Cookies). Flood the head and the gap between the wings with black royal icing. Leave to dry for about ten minutes and then flood the wings with red royal icing. Set the ladybird aside to dry.

BEE
Use the same technique for the bee, outlining and flooding the body with yellow-coloured royal icing. Leave it to dry for about ten minutes, then outline and flood the wings with white royal icing.

BUTTERFLY
First outline and flood the wings with purple-coloured royal icing. Leave to dry a little, then pipe a large dot for the head and a teardrop for the body using very soft peak claret-coloured royal icing. Set aside to dry.

FLOWER
Outline and flood the entire flower shape with pale claret-coloured royal icing and leave to dry.

2 Once the cookies are dry, overpipe with the colours shown in the photograph to form the swirls (see Piping with Royal Icing).

The Princess and the Pea

Whether it's away with the fairies or the delights of Disney, most girls will choose a princess party at least once. When I was little, one of my favourite fairytales was *The Princess and the Pea*, so I enjoyed making a cake to incorporate this idea – not just on the outside, but also by adding 'peas' inside! The bunting topper is easy to make and gives a vintage finishing touch.

You Will Need

MATERIALS

- One 18cm (7in) round, 12cm (4¾in) deep cake (see Cake Recipes) with Perfect Peas effect (optional) (see Inside Cakes), iced in pink sugarpaste (rolled fondant) (see Covering Cakes with Sugarpaste)

- 23cm (9in) round cake drum iced in white sugarpaste at least 12 hours in advance (see Icing Cake Boards)

- Flower (petal/gum) paste: 60g (2¼oz) deep pink, 25g (1oz) white, 15g (½oz) grey

- Lustre dust: pink, silver

- 35g (1¼oz) pea green sugarpaste mixed with 0.75ml (⅛ tsp) CMC (Tylose) (see Modelling Paste and CMC)

EQUIPMENT

- Castellated strip cutter (or small square cutter)

- Frame and crown templates (see Templates)

- 1cm (⅜in) heart cutter

- Two green and white polka dot paper straws or skewers (if preferred)

- 30cm (12in) length of pink and white twine

- Satin ribbon: 45cm (17¾in) length of 1cm (⅜in) pale pink for the bows; 90cm (35½in) length of 1.5cm (⅝in) pink for the base board, plus an additional 15cm (6in) length for the bunting; 15cm (6in) length of 1.5cm (⅝in) green and 7.5cm (3in) length of dark green for the bunting

1 Roll three quarters of the deep pink flower paste into a long 2cm (¾in) thick sausage shape. Use a rolling pin to roll it out into a long, flat piece about 4cm (1¾in) wide and 60cm (24in) long. Press the castellated strip cutter firmly into one side, cutting down the whole length to create the jagged edge. Alternatively a small square cutter can be used to remove squares at even intervals.

2 Use a long sharp knife to cut a parallel straight edge down the other side of the deep pink flower paste. Brush with pink lustre dust using a soft brush, then secure the strip around the base of the cake with edible glue. Neatly trim away the excess icing with a small sharp knife or pair of scissors – the join should be at the back of the cake.

3 Roll out the white flower paste to approximately 1–2mm (¹⁄₁₆in) thick and carefully cut out the frame using the template provided (see Templates). Set it aside. Roll out the remaining pink flower paste to a similar thickness and brush the outer edge with pink lustre dust. Stick the white frame on top of the pink paste with a tiny amount of edible glue and cut around it, leaving an approximately 2mm (¹⁄₁₆in) wide border. Set aside.

4 Thinly roll out the grey flower paste, cut out the crown using the template provided, (see Templates) then brush with silver lustre dust. Use the cutter to remove a heart from the centre of the crown then secure the crown onto the middle of the frame using edible glue. Roll five tiny balls from grey flower paste in the palm of your hand, with one slightly bigger than the rest, and stick them onto the points on the crown with the largest ball in the centre. Carefully attach the frame onto the front of the cake, slightly above the centre.

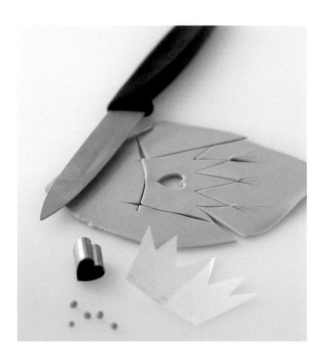

5 Roll tiny pea-sized balls from stiffened pea green sugarpaste in the palm of your hands. Make sure that the paste is nice and pliable to avoid creases. Stick 10 peas randomly onto the base and another 15–20 peas on top of the cake with edible glue, as shown in the photograph.

6 For the bunting topper, secure the twine to the top of each straw (or skewer) using a double knot. Cut two 7.5cm (3in) lengths each from 1.5cm (⅝in) pink and green satin ribbon and one 7.5cm (3in) length from 1.5cm (⅝in) dark green satin ribbon, or use your own desired colours, and cut out a 'V' from each one. Attach a piece of double-sided tape to the plain end of each ribbon then fold them over the twine to secure. Start with the one in the middle and work outwards to ensure the ribbons are evenly spaced. If you prefer, you could use coloured paper strips instead of ribbon. Tie a small, satin ribbon bow to the top of each straw to cover the knots of the twine.

7 Insert the bunting topper in place by pushing the straws (or skewers) into the top of the cake. Finally, secure the 1.5cm (⅝in) pink ribbon around the base board (see Securing Ribbon Around Cakes and Boards).

Extra Inspiration

The crown designs really appeal to little princesses when attached to simple sugarpaste-covered cookie pop treats!

TIP

Show off your baking skills by including green sponge 'peas' inside the cake to really surprise your guests (see Inside Cakes).

Knights of the Round Table

Knights in shining armour coming to the rescue of beautiful princesses makes a perfect boy's alternative or combined (if the girls allow them) party theme. Simply adapt the basic techniques from the main project, changing the colour scheme and embossing the sides of the cake with a brickwork pattern to add extra texture and realism to the castle cakes.

You'll Also Need

- 12.5cm (5in) round, 11.5cm (4½in) deep cake (see Cake Recipes) with Chequered Circles effect (optional) (see Inside Cakes), freshly iced in grey sugarpaste (rolled fondant) (see Covering Cakes with Sugarpaste)

- Brickwork embosser

- Castellated strip cutter (or small square cutter)

- Shield template (see Templates)

- Flower (petal/gum) paste: dark grey, red, black

- Bunting topper made with wooden skewers and 1cm (⅜in) red and black ribbon (see Step 6, The Princess and the Pea)

1 Carefully, but quite firmly, press the brickwork embosser into the soft icing. Work around the base of the cake first then around the top. Use smoothers to help you hold the cake in place if necessary.

2 Use the end of a paintbrush to mark extra lines that have been missed with the brickwork embosser.

3 Roll a strip from the dark grey flower paste, at least 12.5cm (5in) long and 4cm (2¾in) wide, and cut the castellated trim along one edge (see Step 1, The Princess and the Pea). Allow it to dry and stiffen a little before attaching around the top of the cake with edible glue. Make sure that the squares stand upright nicely and don't flop down.

4 Carefully cut out the shield with a sharp knife or scalpel using the template provided (see Templates). To do this, cut out a red and a black shield first then cut through the centre horizontally and vertically for each one. Take two opposite corners from one colour and position them with the alternative opposites of the other colour to reconstruct the shape. Cut out the relevant number from grey flower paste and attach onto the shield with a little edible glue.

5 Roll out the remaining grey flower paste and stick the chequered shield on top with edible glue. Cut around the shape leaving a small border to frame it nicely. Stick the shield to the cake with a small amount of edible glue. Finish by inserting the bunting topper in place by pushing the skewers into the top of the cake.

Extra Inspiration

Downsize and decorate mini cakes (see Mini Cakes) using the same techniques to delight your little knights! Simply decorate the tops of the cakes with shields and helmets using the templates provided (see Templates).

Surf's Up

This tropical-themed cake is perfect for the teenage 'dude' or cool surf 'chick' that likes nothing more than catching a wave or just 'hanging out' at the beach! The colour scheme perfectly captures the essence of hot, summer days and the cake – complete with realistic sand effect – is sure to wow your guests at a summer party or barbeque.

You Will Need

MATERIALS

- Two 28cm (11in) square, approximately 4cm (1½in) deep sponge or chocolate cakes (see Cake Recipes)

- One quantity of buttercream or ganache

- Jam (optional)

- Syrup (optional)

- 1.2kg (2lb 10½oz) white sugarpaste (rolled fondant)

- Edible food colour sprays: red, yellow, orange

- Flower (petal/gum) paste: 10g (¼oz) white, 35g (1¼oz) grey, 20g (¾oz) dark grey

- One packet of crushed light-coloured biscuits (such as Rich Tea)

EQUIPMENT

- Surfboard template (see Templates)

- Two sheets of A4 paper taped together

- Hibiscus stencil (The Creative Cookie Company)

- Two 50 x 35.5cm (20 x 14in) cake boards stuck together with royal icing (see Royal Icing)

- Circle cutters: 6mm (¼in), 1.2cm (½in)

- 3.5m (3¾yd) length of 1.5cm (⅝in) light gold ribbon

1 Shave the crust off the bottom of each 28cm (11in) cake and trim the tops flat to level them. Cut out the surfboard in two pieces from one layer of cake using the template provided (see Templates). Repeat for the second layer.

2 Layer, fill with buttercream or ganache and assemble the four pieces onto the cake board to create a three-dimensional surfboard shape.

3 Round the edges all the way around the surfboard, trying to keep the tip fairly pointed.

4 Cover the cake with buttercream or ganache before placing it in the refrigerator for 20 minutes or so to firm up.

5 Roll out the white sugarpaste to 4mm (⅛in) thick and cover the cake (see Covering with Sugarpaste). Use your hands (and a smoother if necessary) to smooth the icing down and around the sides of the cake and trim away the excess paste with a knife.

6 To make the curved design along the surfboard, carefully place a piece of paper over the cake. Draw a curve running from the bottom right up to the top left below the tip, using the template (see Templates) as a guide. Cut it out and check it fits nicely over the cake. You will need to continue the line so it extends out over the top of the cake. Trim or redraw if necessary.

7 Keep the template on the cake, making sure it is completely flat against the surface – you might like to carefully pin it in place or get someone to help you as you spray. Spray the red food colour spray across the edge of the paper so that it is more concentrated along the cut and tapers off away from it. Carefully remove the paper without smudging and allow to dry.

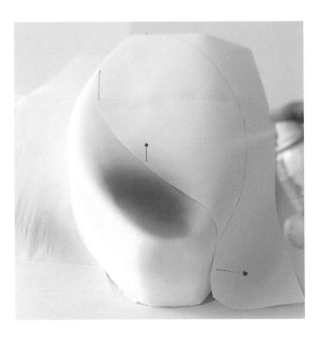

8 Place the hibiscus stencil on the cake towards the middle, right above the curved edge. Protect the area around the stencil with greaseproof (wax) paper, holding it flat against the cake with pins. Use the colour sprays to spray the end of the stamen yellow, then the centre of the flower orange. Lastly, spray the outside of the petals with red to achieve a nice gradient in colour. Carefully remove the stencil.

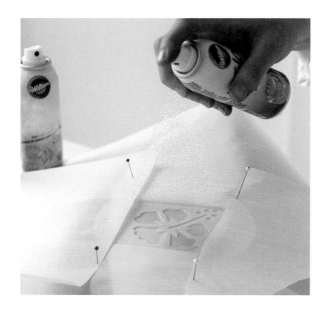

9 To make the leash plug, use the small circle cutter to cut out the sugarpaste. Thinly roll out the white flower paste and use the same cutter to cut a tiny disc to fill the circle. Cut out a circle with the larger circle cutter then take out the centre with the small cutter. Attach it to the cake over the hole. Roll a tiny sausage of grey sugarpaste and stick it inside the hole.

10 To make the cake appear to be sitting on sand, mash up the leftover cake off-cuts with buttercream or ganache and use to build up the area around the surf board until it comes about 2cm (¾in) below the top edge. Taper the slope right to the edge of the cake board. When you have enough height, sprinkle the board with crushed light-coloured biscuits.

11 To make the leash, roll out about a quarter of the grey flower paste to 1mm (¹⁄₁₆in) thick and cut out a rectangular piece, measuring approximately 2 x 1.5cm (¾ x ⅝in). Roll it up lengthways, stick the sides together with some edible glue to hold their shape and then set aside. Roll out the rest of the grey flower paste into a long, narrow shape about 2mm (¹⁄₁₆in) thick and cut out the leash to measure 7 x 1.5cm (2¾ x ⅝in). Form a strap by joining the two ends, with one overlapping the other, and secure with edible glue.

12 Roll a thin sausage of dark grey flower paste to 1–2mm (¹⁄₁₆in) thick and 5cm (2in) long. Cut it in half and insert one end of each piece into the hole made in the board and the other into the small, grey rolled-up piece of paste. Secure with edible glue then attach the grey piece to the surfboard. Roll another slightly thicker 15cm (6in) long sausage from the remaining dark grey flower paste. Trim at both ends and attach one end to the rolled piece of paste on the board and the other to the strap, creating a loop as you do so. The strap can be positioned on the sand to the side of the board.

13 Finish by securing light gold ribbon around the base board (see Securing Ribbon Around Cakes and Boards).

Sand and Surf Cupcakes

These funky little cupcakes are just perfect for a picnic on the beach. Sugarpaste surfboards sit on tempting cupcakes sprinkled with crushed biscuit 'sand'. Use food colour sprays to embellish your boards with fun designs for the ultimate in surfing chic.

You'll Also Need

- Cupcakes (see Baking Cupcakes) in white cases (liners) freshly topped with a caramel-coloured buttercream swirl using a large star nozzle
- Crushed light-coloured biscuits

- White flower (petal/gum) paste
- Surfboard templates (see Templates)
- Edible food colour sprays
- Stencils (optional)

1 Sprinkle the crushed biscuit crumbs onto the freshly topped cupcakes.

2 Roll out the white flower paste to approximately 2mm (¹⁄₁₆in) thick. Use the templates (see Templates) to carefully cut out the surfboards and set them aside on a flat surface to dry out completely.

3 To make the coloured designs, roll out some more white flower paste and cut out curved lines, straight lines, circles and any other desired shapes. Lay them over the dry surfboards and spray them with the food colour sprays. You can either use a single colour or create gradient colour with two or three colour sprays.

4 You can also use a smaller hibiscus flower stencil or any other appropriate small stencil if desired (see Step 8, Surf's Up).

Glitter Glam Mirror Ball

This dazzling design featuring funky dancers, glittering musical notes and a show-stopping mirror ball is ideal for disco divas of any age! Edible glitter and silver leaf transfer sheets make the cake truly glisten and shine. The ball shape is so versatile and can easily be adapted for other designs, such as a football or globe.

You Will Need

MATERIALS

- 280g (10oz) cake batter (see Cake Recipes)

- 350g (12oz) buttercream or ganache

- 18cm (7in) round, 10cm (4in) deep cake (see Cake Recipes), iced in black sugarpaste (rolled fondant) (see Covering with Sugarpaste) and dowelled with three hollow dowels (see Assembling Tiered Cakes)

- 1kg (2lb 4oz) grey sugarpaste

- Round cake drums: 10cm (4in) (or 1cm (⅜in) foam board), 13cm (5in) and 23cm (9in), iced in black sugarpaste (see Icing Cake Boards)

- 60ml (4 tbsp) royal icing coloured with black paste food colouring (see Royal Icing)

- Flower (petal/gum) paste: 100g (3½oz) black, 75g (2¾oz) grey

- 20 silver leaf transfer sheets

- Edible silver glitter

EQUIPMENT

- 15cm (6in) ball tins or two sphere baking moulds (Silverwood)

- 18cm (7in) round tin, lined with baking (parchment) paper (see Preparing Cake Tins)

- Two 5mm (¼in) foam boards: one cut to 15cm (6in) round, one cut to 5cm (2in) round

- Three large straws or thin dowels (see Assembling Tiered Cakes)

- Long skewer

- Cutters: disco dancers, musical notes (Patchwork Cutters)

- Scriber (optional)

- 1m (40in) length of 1.5cm (⅝in) black ribbon

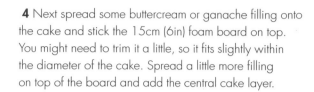

1 To achieve a nice round 15cm (6in) ball cake, I like to bake three separate layers so the cake rises well and cooks quickly and evenly. Grease the ball tin or sphere baking moulds with butter and place them on a tray. You may also need to pop a tiny piece of greaseproof (wax) paper in the ball tin if it has an airhole. Divide the mixture evenly between the two spheres and the 18cm (7in) round tin. Bake for about 20–25 minutes or until cooked (see Cake Recipes). Allow to cool, then wrap and chill for at least a few hours.

> ## TIP
>
> To keep the sphere baking moulds/ball tins upright, scrunch some foil into a sausage shape then shape it into a ring to place around them on the tray.
>
>

2 Trim the two dome cakes so they are flat across the top. Trim around the 18cm (7in) cake with the 15cm (6in) foam board, then shave off the bottom crust and flatten the top. Sit all three pieces together to check you have a rough ball shape and trim the sponge if necessary. Don't worry if the ball appears very slightly short at this stage, as the board and filling will make it taller.

3 Stick the 5cm (2in) foam board to the centre of the underside of one of the domed cakes using ganache or buttercream. Turn the cake up the other way and insert three straws or thin dowels, cut to the depth of the cake, in the centre. Make sure they stay within the area of the foam board underneath.

4 Next spread some buttercream or ganache filling onto the cake and stick the 15cm (6in) foam board on top. You might need to trim it a little, so it fits slightly within the diameter of the cake. Spread a little more filling on top of the board and add the central cake layer.

5 Spread another layer of filling onto the cake and add the top dome cake layer to complete the ball. Use a serrated knife to trim around the whole cake, making sure you have a neat ball shape .

6 Turn the cake upside down and cover the base with the ganache or buttercream filling, spreading it right up to the foam board.

9 Use a knife to mark a horizontal line all the way around the centre of the ball. Attach the squares to the cake, starting around the horizontal line – they should stick by themselves without needing any edible glue; if they don't, use a small amount of sugar syrup. Stick another row of squares below the first, then work all the way around and down to the base of the cake. Use a knife to help tuck the bottom pieces into position at the base of the cake.

7 Turn the cake the right way up and insert a long skewer into the top. This will help you to hold the cake while you coat the top half so the entire ball is covered. Once coated, place the cake in the fridge to firm up. If you are not happy with the shape or the coating is very crumby, apply a second coat of filling. Use a hot palette knife if necessary to get a smooth finish.

8 Mix the grey sugarpaste with a touch of CMC (Tylose) if using soft sugarpaste (see Modelling Paste and CMC). Roll out all the grey sugarpaste to 4mm (⅛in) thick. Cut vertical strips along the sugarpaste, approximately 1cm (⅜in) wide. Now carefully cut 1cm (⅜in) wide horizontal strips across the sugarpaste. This will form 1cm (⅜in) square pieces of icing.

Glitter Glam Mirror Ball | 55

10 Once the bottom half of the ball is covered with grey sugarpaste squares, cover the top, working upwards from the centre in rows. Take the skewer out once you get to the top and place a square right in the centre. Trim pieces of grey sugarpaste to fit neatly around the central top circle.

11 Use the black royal icing to attach the 10cm (4in) iced cake drum onto the 13cm (5in) iced cake drum. Thinly roll out about half of the black flower paste to 40cm (15¾in) long and at least 4cm (1½in) wide. With a sharp knife, cut two 1.5cm (⅝in) wide strips of black flower paste, using a ruler to guide you. Wrap each strip around the two drums and trim them to size, securing them in place with edible glue.

┌─ TIP ─

For extra stability, use foam boards instead of cake drums and pierce a skewer through the entire cake into the platform and the bottom tier. Alternatively, transport the ball and base tier separately, packing some foam or paper cushion around the ball.

14 To apply the silver leaf, first brush the sugarpaste with water so it becomes tacky, then stick a transfer sheet to the cake – you can start anywhere. Use a soft brush to help the silver leaf to adhere then carefully remove the backing.

12 Attach the 18cm (7in) round, 10cm (4in) deep iced cake to the 23cm (9in) drum using royal icing. Roll out the remaining black flower paste into a 55 × 1.5cm (22 × ⅝in) strip and secure it all around the base of the 18cm (7in) cake using edible glue.

13 Secure the ball onto the 10cm (4in) platform with royal icing and allow to dry.

15 Once attached, use a fine paintbrush to carefully tear the leaf in-between the squares to reveal the individual 'mirror' pieces. Continue to apply the silver leaf all over the cake, overlapping the pieces very slightly to avoid gaps. You can cut the transfer sheets when covering smaller areas, rather than having large overlapping pieces. The bottom of the ball is most tricky – use large pieces around this area, working up towards the middle of the cake. As the cake is rounded, the silver leaf will not sit perfectly and will crease and tear a little. Cover the gaps at the end by cutting small pieces of silver leaf and sticking them over the top with a little edible glue.

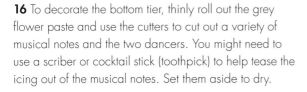

17 Once dry, lay the dancers and musical notes on some greaseproof (wax) paper, paint them with edible glue, then sprinkle them with edible silver glitter. When the dancers and musical notes are completely dry, shake off any excess glitter.

18 Once the cake is assembled in its final position, attach the dancers onto the base cake and the musical notes around the 13in (5in) drum using royal icing.

19 Finish by securing some black ribbon around the base board (see Securing Ribbon Around Cakes and Boards).

TIP

If you would prefer not to use the silver leaf you can just spray or paint the cake with silver lustre, however you won't achieve such a mirror-like effect this way.

Extra Inspiration

Bake some simple cookies (see Baking Cookies), cut out using a star cutter and decorate with edible silver glitter in the same way for a dazzling disco treat!

16 To decorate the bottom tier, thinly roll out the grey flower paste and use the cutters to cut out a variety of musical notes and the two dancers. You might need to use a scriber or cocktail stick (toothpick) to help tease the icing out of the musical notes. Set them aside to dry.

Dazzling Disco Balls

I recently discovered domed foam spheres, which produce perfect sugarpaste coverings, regardless of the height of the cupcakes underneath – genius! They give a professional look to these glitzy disco balls, simply decorated with colourful lights to wow the school disco crowd.

You'll Also Need

- Cupcakes in black or silver foil cases (liners) (see Baking Cupcakes)

- Black sugarpaste (rolled fondant), with a touch of CMC (Tylose) added if the paste is soft (see Modelling Paste and CMC)

- Domed cupcake moulds (Purple Cupcakes)

- Flower (petal/gum) paste: turquoise, orange, red, purple, grey

- Circle cutters: 9cm (3½in), 1.5cm (⅝in)

- Confectioners' glaze

- Piping (pastry) bag and nozzle

- Buttercream

- Silver leaf transfer sheets

DISCO LIGHTS CUPCAKES

1 Roll out the black sugarpaste to 4mm (⅛in) thick, cut out 9cm (3½in) circles and place them over the top of the domed moulds. Leave for a few hours to hold their shape.

2 Roll out the coloured flower pastes to 2mm (¹⁄₁₆in) thick and cut out circles with the 1.5cm (⅝in) cutter. Soften the edges with your finger, attach in place on the domes with edible glue then paint with confectioners' glaze. Allow to dry for five minutes then apply a second coat.

3 Pipe a swirl of buttercream on the cupcake. When dry, sit the domes on top, adjusting the bases if needed.

MIRROR BALL CUPCAKE

1 Cut squares of grey flower paste and cover with silver leaf, trimming away any excess (see Steps 8–9, 14–15, Glitter Glam Mirror Ball).

PAINTBALL PARTY

After a hard day's paintballing, teenagers will love to celebrate with a trendy paintball-themed tiered cake. The camouflage effect that runs through the inside and outside of the cake is sure to impress and the wonky shape of the tiers adds to its style. Have fun adding the graffiti-like 'paint' splatters to the top tier and see if you can hit the target!

YOU WILL NEED

MATERIALS

- 20cm (8in) round, 13cm (5in) deep, and 13cm (5in) round, 11.5cm (4½in) deep cakes (see Cake Recipes) with Cool Camouflage effect (optional) (see Inside Cakes), filled with buttercream/ganache and chilled (see Layering, Filling and Preparation)

- 500g (1lb 2oz) extra buttercream or ganache

- Sugarpaste (rolled fondant): 1kg (2lb 4oz) light green, 200g (7oz) green, brown and black

- Dust colours: bright pink, bright yellow

- Clear alcohol or lemon extract

- 28in (11in) round cake board, iced in brown sugarpaste (see Icing Cake Boards)

- Half quantity of royal icing (see Royal Icing)

- Flower (petal/gum) paste: 670g (11lb 8oz) white, 50g (1¾oz) yellow, bright pink and black

- Paste food colouring: foliage green, black (Sugarflair)

EQUIPMENT

- Round drum or cake card: 20cm (8in), 13cm (5in), 10cm (4in) (optional)

- 15cm (6in) and 9.5cm (3¾in) round, 5mm (¼in) thick pieces of foam board

- Flower cutters

- Cutting wheel

- Multiple-holed piping tube (tip) (No. 234, Wilton)

- Piping (pastry) bag

- Circle cutters: 10cm (4in) (optional), 7.5cm (3in), 7cm (2¾in), 6cm (2⅜in), 4.5cm (1¾in), 3cm (1¼in)

- Tappit number cutters (FMM)

- 1m (40in) length of 1.5cm (⅝in) black ribbon

1 To shape the wonky cake, carefully cut a diagonal slope across the top of the 20cm (8in) round cake. If you are careful and manage to cut through in one clean piece you should be able to flip the cut piece over, placing the thickest part onto the tallest point on the cake. Secure it onto the cake with a thin layer of buttercream and run your knife across the surface of the slope from different angles to make sure it is flat. The angle of the slope is up to you. I like mine to go from just over 13cm (5in) at the highest point to just over 7.5cm (3in) in at the lowest. Place a 20cm (8in) cake drum on top, then flip the cake upside down.

> **TIP**
>
> If you are not confident about getting a clean cut or your cake is very crumbly, keep cutting small slithers away until you achieve a nice slope. You will lose more height to the cake this way, but it's okay. To ensure you have a tall cake, simply bake a deeper cake to start with.

2 Use buttercream to stick the 15cm (6in) round piece of foam board onto the centre of the cake. Start carving down and out towards the 20cm (8in) cake drum to achieve neat, flat sides all the way around the cake (see Carving and Sculpting Cakes). Make sure your knife stays angled outwards – I prefer to work with my knife upright so there is less chance of cutting into the cake.

5 To create the camouflage effect in the icing, first roll out the green, brown and black sugarpaste to 2–3mm (⅛in) thick. Use the flower cutters to cut pieces out from each colour then use a cutting wheel to change the shapes by cutting randomly in half across the petals. Keep the shapes under plastic when you are not using them to prevent them from drying out.

6 Roll out the pale green sugarpaste to about 5mm (¼in) thick. Working quickly, place the coloured cut out shapes onto the paste, keeping the sugarpaste covered around the areas you are not working on. Use a large rolling pin to roll the shapes into the sugarpaste until it is about 3–4mm (⅛in) thick.

3 Flip the cake back up the right way and remove the 20cm (8in) drum. Place a 10cm (4in) drum or cutter in the centre of the cake and make a small cut around it to mark the size. Carefully carve out a flat ledge in the middle of the cake for the top tier to sit into. Do not cut down into the cake on the lower side of the slope; the ledge should taper and meet with the sloping surface at the 10cm (4in) circle mark. When you are happy with the shape, cover it in buttercream and refrigerate to set firm.

4 Repeat Steps 1–3 for the 13cm (5in) top tier, using a 9.5cm (3¾in) round foam board to make the tapered base and omitting the central ledge. Ideally you want to get the cake to 11.5cm (4½in) at the highest point and just under 7.5cm (3in) at the lowest.

7 Cover the 20cm (8in) round cake with the camouflage sugarpaste (see Covering with Sugarpaste), taking extra care around the top edge where the icing is more likely to tear. Cup the sugarpaste gently upwards with your hands to help it stick to the top of the cake and use your fingers to help tease it into the round ledge.

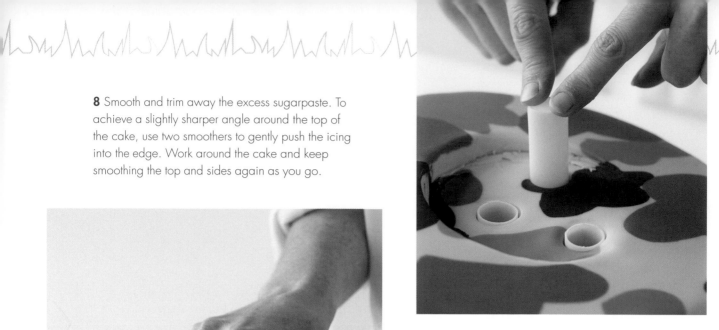

8 Smooth and trim away the excess sugarpaste. To achieve a slightly sharper angle around the top of the cake, use two smoothers to gently push the icing into the edge. Work around the cake and keep smoothing the top and sides again as you go.

9 Repeat Steps 7–8 to cover the top tier with white sugarpaste in the same way. Set the cakes aside for a few hours so the sugarpaste can harden a little, making it easier to handle.

10 Carefully pick up the top tier and check it will fit into the ledge on the bottom tier. If necessary, use a sharp knife to shave off a little icing from inside the ledge. Now dowel the cake (see Assembling Tiered Cakes).

11 Before you assemble the cake you need to decorate the top tier with the paint splat effect. Mix the bright pink dust with clear alcohol or lemon extract so that it is wet enough to flick without being too watery. Wet your flat brush with the 'paint' mixture then, holding the brush fairly close to the cake, pull the bristles back with your finger and let go! Repeat once or twice more in the same place to achieve a denser colour then dab over the centre of the splat very carefully to give the effect of a paintball hitting the area and bursting. Repeat around the cake as much as you like and then continue with the bright yellow colour in the same way. Set aside for about 30 minutes to dry.

12 Attach the bottom tier to the centre of the prepared cake board. Secure the top tier in place using royal icing, making sure the tallest point of the top tier is lined up with the lowest point on the bottom tier.

13 Roll marble-sized balls from yellow, bright pink and black flower paste and use edible glue to secure them in a random order around the base of the top tier. You will need about twelve balls in each colour. Now paint the rolled balls with the pink and yellow dusts mixed with clear alcohol as used in Step 11.

14 Fit the multiple-holed piping tube into a piping bag and fill with stiff foliage green-coloured royal icing (see Colouring Icing). Pipe grass around the bottom tier by simply squeezing out small amounts and pulling away.

15 To make the topper, roll out 20g (¾oz) of black flower paste to 3–4mm (⅛in) thick and cut out a circle with the 4.5cm (2¾in) cutter. Insert a cocktail stick (toothpick) about a third of the way in. Roll out some more black flower paste to 2mm (¹⁄₁₆in) thick and cut out two 7.5cm (3in) circles with the cutter. Thinly roll out the white flower paste and cut out a 7cm (2¾in) circle. Set everything aside to dry.

16 Use the black edible pen and small circle cutters to draw the target onto the white flower paste. Use a ruler to draw in the cross then flick some pink paint onto one side of the disc (see Step 11). Very thinly roll out some black flower paste and cut out the number with the tappit number cutters. Secure it to the centre using edible glue.

17 Stick the pieces of the topper together with black coloured royal icing and set aside to dry. Roll a ball of yellow flower paste, attach it to the centre of the top tier with edible glue and push the topper down inside it, securing it in place with edible glue.

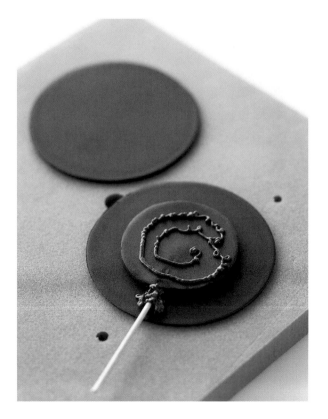

18 Finish by securing some black ribbon around the base board (see Securing Ribbon Around Cakes and Boards).

CAMOUFLAGE CUPCAKES AND COOKIES

If you haven't got time to make the main cake, these cakes and cookies perfectly carry across the camouflage theme with their green and brown royal icing and buttercream coverings, ideal for any teenager's party. The buttercream swirls on the cake can easily be made in any colour – why not try red, yellow and blue for a superhero party?

YOU'LL ALSO NEED

FOR THE CUPCAKES

- Cupcakes (see Baking Cupcakes) in white or black cases (liners) with Cool Camouflage sponge effect (optional) (see Inside Cakes)

- Buttercream: pale green, dark green, chocolate

- Piping (pastry) bags: three medium, one large fitted with piping tube (tip) (Wilton 1M) or large star tip

FOR THE COOKIES

- 10cm (4in) square chocolate cookies (see Baking Cookies),

- Royal icing: pale green for flooding and outlining; dark green, brown and black for piping (see Royal Icing)

- Four piping bags: one fitted with no. 1 piping tube (optional)

2 Close the end of the bag and twist it as usual. Squeeze out some of the icing to test the colours run out nicely before piping a large swirl on top of each cupcake.

COOKIES

1 Fill the piping bag with pale green outlining royal icing and pipe a square to outline the cookie. Flood with the pale green flooding icing (see Royal-Iced Cookies).

2 Fill piping bags with dark green, brown and black royal icings. Working with one colour at a time, drop small 'blobs' into the wet, pale green icing. Set aside to dry.

CUPCAKES

1 To achieve the multi-coloured swirl effect, fill the medium piping bags with the three buttercream colours. Carefully pipe each colour, one at a time, down the sides of the large piping bag. Try to pipe as far down in the bag and as close to the tip as possible, without mixing the colours up.

BIG TOP EXTRAVAGANZA

Children will absolutely love a circus-themed party! Decorate your venue with bright colours and balloons, invite your guests to wear animal or clown-themed fancy dress, and add face painting or perhaps a clown, and you have a winning formula. This simple carved circus tent on a bright and bold platform base will be the real showstopper of the day.

YOU WILL NEED

MATERIALS

- 15cm (6in) round, 7.5cm (3in) deep and 15cm (6in) round, 13cm (5in) deep cakes (see Cake Recipes), both on a thin cake card or 5mm (¼in) foam board, with Piñata Party effect (optional) (see Inside Cakes), layered, filled with buttercream or ganache and chilled (see Layering, Filling and Preparation), or use a 13cm (5in) high, 15cm (6in) base polystyrene cone stuck onto a 15cm (6in) foam board

- 200g (7oz) extra buttercream or ganache

- 1kg (2lb 4oz) white sugarpaste (rolled fondant)

- Flower (petal/gum) paste: 35g (1¼oz) black, 200g (7oz) red, yellow and white, 50g (1¾oz) green, 25g (1oz) blue

- 20cm (8in) round cake, 7.5cm (3in) deep, covered with white sides and blue top (see Panelling Method) and dowelled (see Assembling Tiered Cakes)

- 25cm (10in) cake drum iced in white sugarpaste (see Icing Cake Boards)

EQUIPMENT

- 13cm (5in) round card, board or paper template

- Templates: entrance, side strip, cone strip, flag (see Templates)

- Three straws or thin dowels

- Scallop strip cutter (Jem)

- Star cutters: 2.5cm (1in), 1.5cm (⅝in)

- 1cm (⅜in) circle cutter

- 1m (40in) length of 1.5cm (⅝in) green ribbon

1 To carve the circus tent, place a cocktail stick (toothpick) into the top centre of the 15cm (6in) round, 7.5cm (3in) deep cake. Carve down and out from the cocktail stick to the base until you have a wide cone shape with straight sloping sides (see Carving and Sculpting Cakes). Place it in the fridge to firm up. Alternatively use the cone dummy and stick it to the foam board with royal icing.

TIP

Coat the outside of the cone with ganache to achieve a sharp shape with a firm surface.

---

2 Place the 13in (5in) round card, board or template on top of the 15cm (6in) round, 13in (5in) deep cake. Carve down and out from the card/board to the base to create the tent sides (see Step 1 photograph, Supersize Sprinkle Cupcake). Coat this and the cone, if made from cake, with buttercream or ganache and place in the fridge.

3 Roll out 450g (1lb) of white sugarpaste and use to cover the cone cake/dummy (see Covering with Sugarpaste). Use a smoother to help achieve a flat surface then run it around the base of the cake, perpendicular to the work surface to create an even 4mm (⅛in) flat edge all the way around. Set aside to dry.

4 Cover the bottom part of the tent with the remaining white sugarpaste. Set aside to dry for an hour. Place the entrance template on the front of the cake and cut out the icing. You may need to adjust the template accordingly.

5 Roll out the black flower paste to 2mm (1/16in) thick and use the same template to cut out an entrance shape to insert back into the cake. Smooth the icing with your finger or some leftover paste dusted with cornflour (cornstarch).

6 Thinly roll out 30g (1oz) of red flower paste and cut out the same shape using the entrance template. Again, you may need to adjust your template accordingly. Cut the shape in half vertically down the middle and leave the paste to harden for about five minutes to make it easier to handle. Brush some edible glue onto the outer edge of one of the triangular halves and also onto the cake at the edge of the doorway and carefully attach the red piece in place onto the cake. Gently open back the corner – you may need to hold it in position with the back of a knife for thirty seconds or so to help it adhere in place. Repeat to make the other side of the entrance.

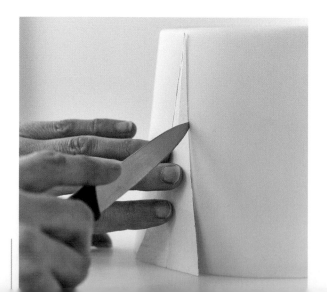

9 Using the cone strip template (see Templates), cut out six red flower paste strips to be placed on the top of the tent. You may need to adjust the size of the strips slightly to suit your cake. Stick them in place with edible glue, trimming them to fit neatly at the top and around the base of the cake.

10 Stick the 20cm (8in) cake onto the cake drum and assemble the tent using three straws or dowels in the bottom tier to support the cone (see Assembling Tiered Cakes). Secure it all in place using royal icing.

11 To make the trim around the top of the tent, first fill in the gaps between the red strips at the base of the cone to allow the scallop border to sit flat. To do this, simply cut tiny strips from white flower paste, trim them to fit in-between the gaps and use edible glue to secure them in place.

7 Thinly roll out about half of the remaining red flower paste. Cut out nine full side strips to go around the tent, using the template (see Templates) as a guide and altering it if necessary to suit the size of your cake. Place one strip at the back of the cake, trim the top and bottom if necessary, and secure it in place with edible glue.

8 Cut out one more red flower paste strip to be positioned above the entrance of the tent. Use the entrance template to cut around the shape of the door, trim to fit if necessary and secure the strip in place with edible glue. Stick four strips on each side of the cake, spacing them evenly apart between the front and back strips already in place.

12 Roll out 30g (1oz) of yellow flower paste to 55cm (22in) long and cut a scallop edge using the scallop strip cutter. Use a long sharp knife to cut a parallel straight edge down the other side of the yellow flower paste, about 1.5cm (⅝in) from the scallop edge (see Step 2, The Princess and the Pea, for a similar method). Roll a marble-sized ball from the remaining yellow flower paste and attach it to the top of the cake with edible glue.

13 To make the flag, roll out about 15g (½oz) of blue flower paste and cut out the curvy shape using the flag template (see Templates). Wrap the flag around the top of a cocktail stick using edible glue and set aside to dry. Stick the flag into the top of the cake using a little edible glue if necessary.

14 To decorate the bottom tier, first calculate the circumference of your cake – it should be about 67–70cm (26–27½in). To work out the width of your triangles, divide the circumference by eight; the height of the triangles will be the height of your cake. Create a triangular template to these measurements.

15 Thinly roll out the yellow and white flower paste and use your template to cut out eight triangles from each colour. Stick them onto the cake with the yellow triangles pointing upwards and the white triangles pointing downwards. Use the smaller star cutter to cut out a star from leftover white flower paste and attach it above the entrance of the tent with edible glue.

TIP

Cut the triangles slightly larger than you need and trim as you stick them around the cake to make sure they fit exactly.

16 Thinly roll out just over half of the green flower paste, use the larger star cutter to cut out a star for each of the white triangles and stick them in place with edible glue. Roll out some of the leftover red flower paste, use the circle cutter to cut out a dot for each of the yellow triangles and stick them in place using edible glue.

17 For the balloons, roll three 15g (½oz) balls from blue, yellow and green flower paste and shape them into cones. Stick the yellow balloon onto the cake first with edible glue. Insert a cocktail stick through the middle to hold it in place and help secure the green balloon. Stick the blue balloon on next, applying a small amount of glue to the yellow balloon as well as to the cake. Lastly, attach the green balloon over the cocktail stick.

18 Roll three tiny balls from blue, yellow and green flower paste, shape them into cones with a flat bottom and attach them with edible glue to the pointed end of each balloon. Roll three very thin sausage pieces of white flower paste for the strings. Carefully attach one end to each balloon and the other end to the entrance so they appear to be coming out of the tent. Use a knife to neatly trim the excess paste and a paintbrush to help you position everything in place.

19 Finish by securing some green ribbon around the base board (see Securing Ribbon Around Cakes and Boards).

TIP

Make sure you remove all the cocktail sticks from the cake before serving.

CRAZY CLOWN CUPCAKES

These fun clown face cupcakes are guaranteed to make the children smile! I have given instructions for two designs but you can have fun making different expressions, varying the accessories and using a wide range of bright colours to make truly characterful cupcakes.

YOU'LL ALSO NEED

- Cupcakes (see Baking Cupcakes) in coloured foil cupcake cases (liners), covered in flesh coloured sugarpaste (rolled fondant) (see Covering Cupcakes with Sugarpaste)

- Flower (petal/gum) paste: green, white, yellow, pink, blue, purple, red, black

- Circle cutters: 1.5cm (⅝in), 3cm (1¼in), 3.5cm (1⅜in)

- Cutting wheel (optional)

- 1.5cm (⅝in) heart cutter

- 4cm (1½in) five-petal blossom cutter

CLOWN WITH GREEN HAT

1 For the hat, cut out a disc of 4mm (⅛in) thick green flower paste with the 3.5cm (1⅜in) circle cutter and shape it into an oval. Roll a 5 x 0.5cm (2 x ¼in) sausage shape for the rim, then cut a section from the hat piece and stick the rim in place. Use a cocktail stick (toothpick) to hold the hat in position until it is secure.

2 For the eyes, thinly roll out some white flower paste and cut out two 1.5cm (⅝in) circles. Elongate the eyes to form ovals and use the same cutter to take out the bottom sections. Roll eight tiny black flower paste teardrops and attach in place on the eyes.

3 For the mouth, use the 3.5cm (1⅜in) cutter to cut out some thinly rolled white flower paste then use the same cutter to take out the top section. Use a knife or cutting wheel to round off the two sides neatly. Roll a small sausage piece of red flower paste, taper each end slightly and flatten a little. Use the 3.5cm (1⅜in) cutter to indent the smile and go over the curve with a black edible pen.

4 Roll a pea-sized ball of red flower paste for the nose and two tiny flattened pink balls for cheeks. For the hair, cut out 3mm (⅛in) thick yellow flower paste with the blossom cutter and cut roughly in half. Secure with edible glue.

CLOWN WITH YELLOW HAT

1 For the hat, roll yellow flower paste to 3mm (⅛in) thick, cut out a 3.5 x 3cm (1⅜ x 1¼in) triangle and stick it in place.

2 Make the white areas for the eyes and mouth, and form the nose as before. Roll two tiny tapered black flower paste sausages to stick on top of the eyes. Use the 1.5cm (⅝in) cutter to cut two tiny half moon shapes from blue flower paste for eyebrows and attach with edible glue.

3 For the lips, use the heart cutter to cut a heart from 2mm (1/16in) thick red flower paste, then use the circle cutter to adjust the shape and indent the smile. Roll two tiny red balls for either side of the mouth and draw a curve with edible black pen. For the hair, roll various pea-sized balls of pink, green and purple flower paste and attach with edible glue.

Supersize Sprinkle Cupcake

Giant cupcakes are so simple and fun to make, not just for children's parties but for adult celebrations too! I like to cover the top in sugarpaste and carve out a traditional swirl, but you could just as easily create a buttercream peak or dome with a palette knife. Once decorated with pretty sprinkles, it will look impressive whichever way you choose.

You Will Need

MATERIALS

- Two 18cm (7in) round, 4.5cm (1¾in) deep cakes (see Cake Recipes): one for the cupcake base and one for the top, layered and filled with buttercream or ganache (see Layering, Filling and Preparation)

- 350g (12oz) buttercream or ganache for coating the cakes

- Sugarpaste (rolled fondant): 700g (1lb 9oz) powder blue-coloured (mix blue with a touch of purple), 500g (1lb 2oz) white

- Quarter quantity of royal icing (see Royal Icing)

- Flower (petal/gum) paste: 10g (¼oz) pink, 10g (¼oz) slightly darker pink, 20g (¾oz) very pale pink

- Pearl white lustre dust

- 25cm (10in) cake drum iced in dusky pink sugarpaste (see Icing Cake Boards)

EQUIPMENT

- 18cm (7in) and 15cm (6in) pieces of 5mm (¼in) foam board or thin cake card

- Three dowels or large straws, at least 15cm (6in) long (see Assembling Tiered Cakes)

- 5cm (2in) heart cutter

- Small piping (pastry) bag

- 1m (40in) length of 1.5cm (⅝in) dusky pink ribbon

1 Start by carving the base of the cupcake. Sit one of the cakes on the 18cm (7in) foam board or cake card and stick the 15cm (6in) board/card centrally on top using buttercream or ganache. Carefully carve a sloping edge all the way around the cake from the 15cm (6in) board/card down to the 18cm (7in) one (see Carving and Sculpting Cakes). Make sure you keep your blade angled outwards to avoid cutting into the base too much. Once you have made the first cuts all the way around, trim and neaten the shape by going around the cake with the knife held upwards.

2 Cover the cake in buttercream or ganache (see Layering, Filling and Preparation). Remove the 18cm (7in) base card/board and place the cake on a chopping board or flat plate before placing it in the fridge to firm up for about 20 minutes. If your cake is crumbly, you may need to neaten the surface with a second coat of buttercream or ganache.

3 Next carve the top of the cupcake. Place the other 18cm (7in) round cake onto the 18cm (7in) board/card and make a little mark in the centre top of the cake with a knife. Carve out a pointed dome-like shape, cutting down from the central mark at the top of the cake to the 18cm (7in) base.

4 Once you have a neat, even shape, use an edible pen or knife to mark a swirl, starting from the top and going around and down to the bottom. Start carving out the swirl with a small sharp knife. If you aren't confident, first make a small indentation only, then carve more of the cake out little by little. Use your hands to help shape the sponge – press in the indents with your fingers and brush off the crumbs.

5 Carefully coat the cake in a thin layer of buttercream or ganache and place it in the fridge to chill for 20 minutes.

6 Place the cupcake base on some greaseproof (wax) paper, still upside down with the 15cm (6in) card or board on top, and cover with the blue sugarpaste (see Covering with Sugarpaste). Carefully slice off the top of the sugarpaste to reveal the card underneath.

7 Use the flat side of a cake smoother to make indentations in the soft icing all the way around the cake. Turn the cake up the right way and set aside.

8 Cover the swirl cake in white sugarpaste, using your hands to smooth the icing into the grooves of the swirl.

> **TIP**
>
> Use a small piece of sugarpaste dusted with cornflour (cornstarch) to help smooth the sugarpaste for a better finish.

9 Dowel the base cake (see Assembling Tiered Cakes) and secure onto the prepared cake drum with royal icing. Attach the swirl cake on top with buttercream or ganache.

10 Roll out the pink flower paste to 3mm (⅛in) thick and use the cutter to cut out the heart topper. Set aside to dry. Roll a long, thin sausage from darker pink flower paste and cut 1cm (⅜in) pieces for the sprinkles (sugar strands). Roll marble-sized balls of pale pink flower paste for the dragées (sugar balls) and dust everything with pearl lustre.

11 Use a small piping bag filled with royal icing to attach the heart topper and sprinkles onto the cupcake and drum. Finally, secure some dusky pink ribbon around the cake drum (see Securing Ribbon Around Cakes and Boards).

Sweet Cupcake Cookies

These pastel cupcake cookies are the perfect sweet treat! I was inspired by the wallpaper background in the Supersize Sprinkle Cupcake photograph and created a few cute variations from this. You can easily experiment by changing the colour scheme, adding shop-bought sprinkles and dragées, or even have fun making your own.

You'll Also Need

- Vanilla cupcake cookies (see Baking Cookies)

- Royal icing (see Royal Icing)

- Paste food colouring: claret, blue, purple

- Small and large piping (pastry) bags

- No. 1 piping tubes (tips)

- Pink and white heart sprinkles (sugar strands)

- Pink mimosa balls

- Pink pearl dragées (sugar balls)

1 Start by colouring the royal icing (see Colouring Icing). You will need two bags per colour: one for outlining and one for flooding. Use claret for the pink and mix blue with a touch of purple for the powder blue colour.

BLUE-TOPPED CUPCAKE
1 Outline and flood the case (liner) with pink icing (see Royal-Iced Cookies), making a small scalloped edge along the top. Leave to dry for about ten minutes, then outline and flood the top with blue icing.

2 When dry, overpipe the details on the case with white icing (see Piping with Royal Icing). Pipe a white zigzag down and across from the top, add pale pink dots and top with a white heart sprinkle.

PINK-TOPPED CUPCAKE
1 Outline and flood the case in white with a zigzag top edge, then outline and flood the top in pink.

2 When dry, overpipe the details on the case then outline and flood the cream topping with white icing. Leave to dry, then pipe on pink and pale pink dots, attach a mimosa ball to the top and add dragées using royal icing.

WHITE-TOPPED CUPCAKE
1 Outline and flood the case in blue with a large scalloped top edge, then outline and flood the top in white.

2 Overpipe the details on the case with white icing. Pipe tiny pink dots and attach heart sprinkles using royal icing.

Pretty Print Vanity Case

From tweens to teens, girls of any age love make-up and this pink and black vanity case is right in vogue! The leopard-print design is great fun to make by simply stamping sugarpaste shapes onto the cake. Complete the look with modelled make-up in the latest shades to add a touch of glitz and glamour to a girly party.

You Will Need

MATERIALS

- 25cm (10in) round, 11cm (4¼in) deep dense cake made with 10% extra flour (see Cake Recipes) with designer leopard-print effect (optional) (see Inside Cakes), layered and filled with buttercream or ganache and chilled (see Layering, Filling and Preparation)

- Sugarpaste (rolled fondant): 700g (1lb 9oz) pink, 1.25kg (2lb 12oz) slightly paler pink

- Flower (petal/gum) paste: 50g (1¾oz) grey, 75g (2¾oz) black, 75g (2¾oz) pale pink, 20g (¾oz) cerise pink (or modelling paste), 5g (⅛oz) purple

- Lustre dust: pink, silver, lilac or pearl

- Black paste food colouring

- 33cm (13in) cake drum iced in ivory sugarpaste (see Icing Cake Boards)

- Quarter quantity of royal icing (see Royal Icing)

- Lemon extract or clear alcohol

EQUIPMENT

- Straws or dowels (optional)

- Long metal ruler

- Stitching tool

- Strip cutter (Straight Frill Set 1–4, FMM)

- Firm bristled brush

- 20 x 11cm (8 x 4¼in) piece of 5mm (¼in) foam board,

- Circle cutters: 4.5cm (1¾in), 3.5cm (1⅜in)

- 110cm (44in) length of 1.5cm (⅝in) dusky pink ribbon

1 Form the case shape by cutting off a section from the round cake to form a flat base that the cake can stand upright upon. The more cake you cut off, the easier it is to achieve a sturdy base; although you will lose some of the overall effect, and more of your cake! Cover the cake in buttercream or ganache and place it in the fridge for 20 minutes or so to firm up.

TIP

If your cake is very soft, especially if you are using buttercream rather than ganache, you might like to put some foam board in the centre of the cake and add some dowels or straws to give it support (see Assembling Tiered Cakes).

---

2 Roll out the pink sugarpaste to 60 x 13cm (23½ x 5in) and use to cover the top section of the cake (see Covering with Sugarpaste). Use a smoother to help the icing to stick well, then carefully trim away the excess icing on both sides with a sharp knife to leave a clean, neat edge.

3 Use a metal ruler to mark an indent just over 2.5cm (1in) into one side to show where the lid meets the base. Carefully roll the ruler over the surface, rather than dragging it.

4 Roll out two-thirds of the pale pink sugarpaste and cut a straight edge down one side. Lift the paste up with the rolling pin and cover one side of the bag, draping the icing over the top. Trim neatly around the top edge. Repeat for the other side, then set the cake aside for a few hours or overnight so the icing can dry a little.

5 To make the stamps for the leopard-print, simply roll about twelve different-sized pieces of pale pink sugarpaste into uneven sausage shapes. Curve them and taper the ends slightly, then flatten one side a little to enable them to stand upright. Set aside to dry.

6 It is best to make the handle 24 hours in advance. Roll out some pale pink flower paste to 3–4mm (⅛in) thick and 30 x 3.25cm (12 x 1⅛in) in size. Trim the ends and sides to create a perfectly straight strip of icing, then fold over both ends inwards and use the stitching tool to mark each end of the handle. Set aside to dry out completely.

7 Use a soft brush to dust faint stripes of pink lustre onto the sides of the vanity case. Next, dust on splodges on the sides – these will be the centres of the black leopard-print pattern.

8 Put some black paste food colouring into a pot or dish and add a touch of water to dilute it if necessary, making it easier to paint with. Paint the flat side of the sugarpaste sausage shapes and stamp them onto the cake around the darker areas of lustre dust to create a leopard-print pattern. You can paint and stamp each shape about fives times before it become too soggy and unusable.

TIP

One of my fellow crafty tutors, Erin Gardner, uses pieces of dried celery instead of sugarpaste to stamp similar shapes.

Test your paint consistency first on a piece of paper or sugarpaste.

9 Use a soft brush to touch up the prints on the cake to create a more fur-like effect. Repeat until you are happy with the amount of detail on the cake, then secure the cake onto the cake drum using royal icing.

10 Thinly roll out the black flower paste to 60cm (23½in) long. Use the strip cutter down one side to cut down the whole length of the paste. With a long sharp knife, carefully cut a parallel straight edge down the other side of the black flower paste (see Step 2, The Princess and the Pea, for a similar method) then cut in half to form two strips. Use edible glue to attach the strips to each side, placing the straight edges against each patterned side.

11 To make the handle elements, roll out about half of the grey flower paste to 3mm (⅛in) thick and cut two 4.25 x 1.25cm (1⅝ x ½in) pieces. Roll four tiny sausages, trim them to 1.5cm (⅝in) long and bend them at a right angle. Stick the handle onto the rectangular pieces of paste with edible glue, then attach them together onto the cake. Push the sausage clasp pieces into either side of the handle loop to join the grey plate, attaching them in place with edible glue.

TIP

For a really wild effect, bake the sponge with a leopard-print design (see Inside Cakes).

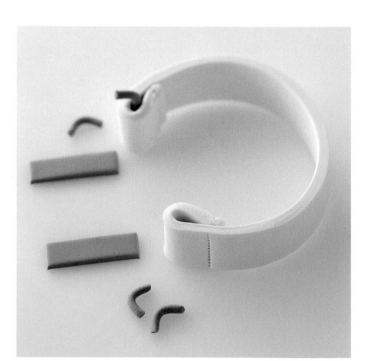

12 To make the clasp, roll out some more grey flower paste to 4mm (⅛in) thick and cut out two pieces measuring 2.5 x 1.25cm (1 x ½in). Stick them onto the cake on either side of the lid opening line. Roll two more small sausages shapes, about 5mm (¼in) in length for the press clasp and attach to either side of the main rectangular clasp piece. Paint the grey flower paste with silver lustre dust mixed with clear alcohol to add shine.

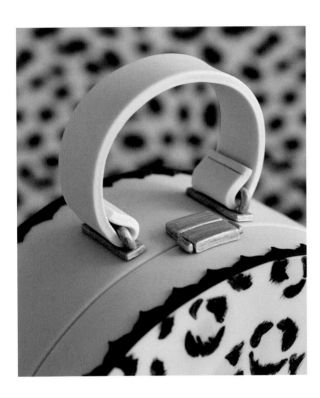

13 To make the nail varnish, roll a 7 x 1.5cm (2¾ x 5in) sausage shape from black flower paste and slightly taper it at one end to form the lid. Roll a ball from the cerise pink flower paste or modelling paste and form it into a fat cone shape before flattening the end to make the base. Stick the lid on top with edible glue and set aside to dry, ensuring that the lid remains in an upright position.

> TIP
>
> Experiment by creating additional make-up items, such as lipstick and blusher, from sugarpaste to fill your board with treats!

14 To make the eye shadow, cut a 1.25cm (½in) and a 1cm (⅜in) thick disc from black flower paste using the 4.5cm (1¾in) circle cutter. Shape the top edge of the thinner disc with your fingers to form the lid. Mark indents around the top edge of the base disc with a sharp knife.

15 Cut out a 2mm (¹⁄₁₆in) thick disc from purple flower paste with the 3.5cm (1⅜in) cutter and soften the top edge with your finger. Dust it with lilac or pearl lustre and secure the eye shadow to the base with edible glue. Stick the make-up on top of the cake board using royal icing.

16 Finish by securing some dusky pink ribbon around the base board (see Securing Ribbon Around Cakes and Boards).

Heaven Scent Mini Cakes

For the ultimate in luxury, shape mini cakes into little balls and decorate with decorative silver lids to make opulent perfume bottles. The zebra-print design is simple to paint onto the white sugarpaste base and makes a real fashion statement that girls will adore.

You'll Also Need

- Ball-shaped mini cake (7.5cm (3in) sphere baked in two halves, sandwiched together with filling then coated and chilled) (see Mini Cakes)

- White sugarpaste (rolled fondant)

- Pink lustre spray

- Grey flower (petal/gum) paste

- Rolling pins: daisy-textured, smooth

- Six-petal flower cutters: 8.5cm (3⅜in), 4cm (1½in)

- 5cm (2in) cake card

- Silver lustre dust

- 13cm (5in) cake drum, iced in white sugarpaste (see Icing Cake Boards) and painted with zebra-print pattern using black paste food colouring

1 Roll out the white sugarpaste and cover the chilled ball cake, using your hands to cup the icing around the cake and down to the base. Trim away the excess paste and smooth the icing with the palm and heel of your hand. Lightly spray the icing with pink lustre spray to add a gentle shine here and there.

2 Roll out some grey flower paste to 2mm (¹⁄₁₆in) thick with a smooth rolling pin, then roll the daisy-textured rolling pin over the top, pressing down firmly to reveal a floral pattern in the paste.

3 Cut out a flower shape from the daisy-patterned grey flower paste with the 8.5cm (3⅜in) six-petal flower cutter for the lid, then brush with silver lustre dust. Attach onto the top of the ball cake using edible glue.

4 To make the lid, roll a sausage of grey flower paste to 1.5cm (⅝in) thick and cut it to 1.5cm (⅝in) in length. Dust it with silver lustre and attach it to the centre of the grey flower paste with edible glue. Roll out some more grey flower paste to 5mm (¼in) thick, cut out another flower shape with the 4cm (1½in) cutter and secure to the top of the lid with edible glue.

5 Stick the bottle onto the painted board with royal icing or buttercream and wrap some pink ribbon around it (see Attaching Ribbon Around Cakes and Boards).

Superhero Cityscape

Almost every child has a favourite superhero growing up, and a themed party gives them the perfect opportunity to dress up as their idol for the day! With this pop art, comic strip-style cityscape cake – complete with bright colours, bold stars and an age exclamation bubble – they can really get into character and imagine they are saving the city from danger!

You Will Need

MATERIALS

- 13cm (5in) round, 11.5cm (4½in) deep cake and 18cm (7in) round, 13cm (5in) deep cake (see Cake Recipes) with Piñata Party effect (optional) (see Inside Cakes), layered, filled and coated with buttercream or ganache and chilled (see Layering, Filling and Preparation)

- Flower (petal/gum) paste: 200g (7oz) white, 200g (7oz) black, 75g (2¾oz) red, 60g (2¼oz) blue

- One 23cm (9in) cake drum iced in black sugarpaste (rolled fondant) (see Icing Cake Boards)

- Sugarpaste: 450g (1lb) yellow, 1.25kg (2lb 12oz) white

- Edible icing sheets: one blue with darker blue dots, two yellow with orange dots (see Edible Icing Sheets)

- Quarter quantity of royal icing (see Royal Icing)

EQUIPMENT

- Three dowels cut to size (see Assembling Tiered Cakes)

- Templates: outer and inner exclamation bubbles, skyscrapers (see Templates)

- 3cm (1¼in) star cutter

- 75cm (28in) length of 1.5cm (⅝in) black ribbon

1 Start by making the number exclamation bubble so it can dry out completely before attaching it to the cake. Roll out about half of the white flower paste to approximately 2–3mm (⅛in) thick and carefully cut around the outer exclamation bubble template (see Templates). Place the inner exclamation bubble template (see Templates) on the blue dotty edible icing sheet and draw around it using a black edible pen. Cut out the shape outside the black outline with a scalpel and ruler or a sharp pair of scissors. Stick the dotted piece onto the white flower paste using a small amount of edible glue and set aside to dry.

3 Cover the 18cm (7in) round cake in the same way as in Step 2, then dowel the cake (see Assembling Tiered Cakes). Assemble both tiers on the prepared cake drum.

4 Accurately measure the height of the top tier. Measure and mark up this length along the width of one of the yellow dotty edible icing sheets. Carefully cut across this width to create a strip to wrap around the top tier. You may need to trim the sheet first if there are any rounded corners. Brush a small amount of edible glue onto the cake and attach the edible icing sheet.

─ TIP ─

It is a good idea to make two exclamation bubble number toppers, just in case one gets damaged!

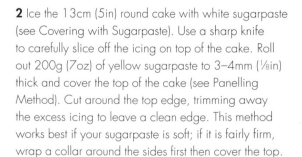

2 Ice the 13cm (5in) round cake with white sugarpaste (see Covering with Sugarpaste). Use a sharp knife to carefully slice off the icing on top of the cake. Roll out 200g (7oz) of yellow sugarpaste to 3–4mm (⅛in) thick and cover the top of the cake (see Panelling Method). Cut around the top edge, trimming away the excess icing to leave a clean edge. This method works best if your sugarpaste is soft; if it is fairly firm, wrap a collar around the sides first then cover the top.

5 Use the second icing sheet to cover the rest of the top tier, measuring and trimming accurately first and securing with edible glue, as in Step 4. You won't need the full length of the sheet this time. Make sure the pattern matches up on one side – it won't match up on the other, so this will become the back of the cake.

6 Use the leftover side of the yellow edible icing sheet to wrap around the top of the 18cm (7in) tier. You will need to use the leftover piece from the second top tier strip to finish covering the cake.

7 Thinly roll out the black flower paste and cut out skyscraper silhouettes in different shapes and sizes with a sharp knife. I have given a couple of example templates (see Templates) to help get you started. Start by cutting basic rectangular shapes: the buildings should be 10–13cm (4–5in) tall and 1.5–3cm (⅝–1¼in) wide. Cut out corners from some of the shapes to add interest. Secure the silhouettes to the bottom tier with a little edible glue, leaving a 4–8mm (⅛–⁵⁄₁₆in) gap between each one.

8 Thinly roll out the red, blue and remaining white flower paste and cut out slightly smaller skyscrapers to be positioned in front of the black ones. You will need about six of each colour, along with any handy spares! Cut out two stars using the star cutter and cut the required number freehand from the remaining red flower paste. Set everything aside to dry on a flat surface.

9 Use the edible black pen and a ruler to colour around the edges of the stars and number. Next outline the top and sides of each skyscraper and draw in simple windows and building feature details. You can attach some leftover edible blue icing sheets onto the blue skyscrapers using edible glue and outline with edible pen if desired. Try to make each skyscraper different to add interest to the design.

10 Stick the skyscrapers onto the cake with royal icing, alternating the colours as you go.

11 Secure the number to the exclamation bubble with small amount of royal icing and attach it to the cake. To make sure it is well secured, tear away a little of the yellow edible icing sheet from the top tier first and stick the exclamation bubble directly onto to the sugarpaste. Finally attach the two red stars directly onto the yellow edible icing sheet on the top tier.

12 Finish by securing some black ribbon around the base board (see Attaching Ribbon Around Cakes and Boards).

Magnificent Mask Cookies

These colourful mask cookies are a great addition to a superhero party. I have included a few different character designs, but feel free to experiment to make your own favourites. You can even cut holes on either side of the cookies and thread ribbon or elastic through to enable your little heroes to have fun trying them on!

You'll Also Need

- Vanilla mask cookies (see Baking Cookies) cut from templates (see Templates)

- Royal icing (see Royal Icing)

- Paste food colouring: foliage green, baby blue, black, red, yellow and ivory (Sugarflair)

- Small and large piping (pastry) bags

- No. 1 piping tubes (tips)

1 Start by colouring the royal icing (see Colouring Icing). You will need two bags of each colour: one for outlining and one for flooding. To make the grey-coloured royal icing, use a small amount of black paste food colouring.

2 Outline and flood all the cookies (see Royal-Iced Cookies). For the cookies flooded with more than one colour, make sure you allow your first colour to dry for about ten minutes before flooding in the next colour.

3 Allow all the flooding icing to dry before overpiping the details, using the photograph as a reference (see Piping with Royal Icing). For the Hulk mask, use very soft peak black icing to outline and flood the hair.

Recipes and Techniques

CAKE RECIPES

Always source the best quality ingredients for a superior flavour and to ensure your cakes taste as amazing as they look. For a professional, crust-free finish every time, bake your cakes in a tin that is 2.5cm (1in) larger than the required final dimensions. The sizes and quantities specified in the charts that follow in this section will make cakes that are about 7.5–9cm (3–3½in) deep. For shallower cakes and mini cakes, use smaller quantities (see Mini Cakes).

Measuring in Cups

If you prefer to use US cup measurements, please use the following conversions:

Liquid

- 1 tsp = 5ml
- 1 tbsp = 15ml (or 20ml for Australia)
- ½ cup = 120ml/4fl oz
- 1 cup = 240ml/8½fl oz

Caster (superfine) sugar/brown sugar

- ½ cup = 100g/3½oz
- 1 cup = 200g/7oz

Butter

- 1 tbsp = 15g/½oz
- 2 tbsp = 25g/1oz
- ½ cup/1 stick = 115g/4oz
- 1 cup/2 sticks = 225g/8oz

Icing (confectioners') sugar

- 1 cup = 115g/4½oz

Flour

- 1 cup = 125g/4½oz

Sultanas (golden raisins)

- 1 cup = 165g/5¾oz

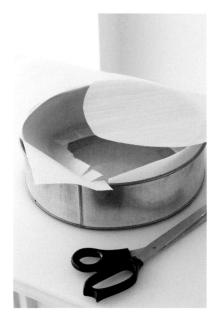  

Preparing Cake Tins

To prevent your cake from sticking to the baking tin (pan) I prefer to line the bottom and sides of the tin well before adding the cake mixture and baking.

1 To line the bottom of round cake tins, lay your tin on a piece of greaseproof (wax) paper or baking (parchment) paper and draw around it using an edible pen. Using scissors, cut around the inside of the line so that the circle will be a good fit, and put aside. Cut a long strip of the paper at least 9cm (3½in) wide, fold over one of the long sides by 1cm (⅜in) and crease firmly, then open out. Cut slits from the edge nearest to the fold up to the fold, with each slit about 2.5cm (1in) apart. Put the strip around the inside of tin, with the fold tucked into the bottom corner, then add the greaseproof paper circle and smooth down.

2 For square cakes, lay a piece of greaseproof or baking paper over the top of the tin. Cut a square that overlaps it on each side by 7.5cm (3in). Cut a slit at each end on two opposite sides. Push the paper inside the tin and tuck the flaps behind.

CAKE PORTION GUIDE

The following chart indicates approximately how many portions will be made by the different cake sizes. The number specified is based on each portion being about 2.5cm (1in) square and 9cm (3½in) deep.

Size	10cm (4in)		13cm (5in)		15cm (6in)		18cm (7in)		20cm (8in)		23cm (9in)		25cm (10in)		28cm (11in)	
Shape	○	Sq	○	Sq	○	Sq	○	Sq	○	Sq	○	Sq	○	Sq	○	Sq
Portions	5	10	10	15	20	25	30	40	40	50	50	65	65	85	85	100

Classic Sponge Cake

I have used one basic sponge recipe for all the cakes in this book – this classic recipe is so simple to bake and pleases the children every time! I have also provided flavour alternatives if you want to vary the taste (see Additional Flavourings). Separate the mixture between two tins to ensure that your sponge cake is really light. If you want to make three layers, split the mixture one-third/two-thirds. For smaller cakes, you can also cut three layers of sponge from a larger square cake. For example, a 15cm (6in) round cake can be cut from a 30cm (12in) square cake (see Note (above chart) and also Layering, Filling and Preparation).

TIP

Ensure that your butter and eggs are at room temperature before you start.

---

1 Preheat your oven to 160°C/325°F/Gas Mark 3 and line your tins (pans) (see Preparing Cake Tins).

2 In a large electric mixer, beat the butter and sugar together until light and fluffy. Add the eggs gradually, beating well between each addition, then add the flavouring.

3 Sift the flour, add to the mixture and mix very carefully until just combined.

4 Remove the bowl from the mixer and fold the mixture through gently with a spatula to finish. Tip the mixture into your prepared tin or tins and spread with a palette knife or the back of a spoon.

5 Bake in the oven until a skewer inserted into the centre of your cakes comes out clean. The baking time will vary depending on your oven. Check small cakes after 20 minutes and larger cakes after 40 minutes.

6 Leave to cool, then wrap the cake in cling film (plastic wrap) and refrigerate until ready to use.

DEEPER CAKES

For deeper cakes, simply bake up to one and a half times the recipe. You may need to bake this in two batches if you only have a couple of tins. Leave the cakes to cool slightly before turning them out and refilling the tins with the mixture.

SHELF LIFE

Sponges should be made up to 24 hours in advance. Freeze them if they are not being used the next day. After the one to two day processes of layering and covering the cakes, the finished cakes should last for up to three to four days out of the fridge.

Note: If cutting three layers from a larger square cake: for a 15cm (6in) round cake, bake an 8 egg/400g (14oz) butter etc. mix in a 30cm (12in) square tin; for a 13cm (5in) round or square cake, bake a 7 egg/350g (12oz) mix in a 28cm (11in) square tin; for a 10cm (4in) round or square cake, bake a 6 egg/300g (10½oz) mix in a 25cm (10in) square tin. Add five to ten per cent extra flour for deeper tiers and carved cakes, or if you find that your sponges are too soft to work with.

Cake size round square	13cm (5in) 10cm (4in)	15cm (6in) 13cm (5in)	18cm (7in) 15cm (6in)	20cm (8in) 18cm (7in)	23cm (9in) 20cm (8in)	25cm (10in) 23cm (9in)	28cm (11in) 25cm (10in)	30cm (12in) 28cm (11in)
Unsalted butter	150g (5½oz)	200g (7oz)	250g (9oz)	325g (11½oz)	450g (1lb)	525g (1lb 3oz)	625g (1lb 6oz)	800g (1lb 12oz)
Caster (superfine) sugar	150g (5½oz)	200g (7oz)	250g (9oz)	325g (11½oz)	450g (1lb)	525g (1lb 3oz)	625g (1lb 6oz)	800g (1lb 12oz)
Medium eggs	3	4	5	6	9	10	12	14
Vanilla extract (tsp)	½	1	1	1½	2	2	2½	4
Self-raising (-rising) flour	150g (5½oz)	200g (7oz)	250g (9oz)	325g (11½oz)	450g (1lb)	525g (1lb 3oz)	625g (1lb 6oz)	800g (1lb 12oz)

ADDITIONAL FLAVOURINGS

Lemon Add the finely grated zest of one lemon per 100g (3½oz) of sugar.

Orange Add the finely grated zest of two oranges per 250g (9oz) of sugar.

Chocolate Replace 15g (½oz) of flour with 15g (½oz) of cocoa powder (unsweetened cocoa) per 100g (3½oz) of flour.

Banana Replace the caster (superfine) sugar with brown sugar. Add one mashed overripe banana and ½ teaspoon mixed spice (apple pie spice) per 100g (3½oz) of flour.

Coffee and walnut Replace 15g (½oz) of flour with 15g (½oz) of finely chopped walnuts per 100g (3½oz) of flour. Replace the caster sugar with brown sugar and add cooled shots of espresso coffee to taste.

INSIDE CAKES

Designs and colourful patterns inside the cake itself have become all the rage over the last few years, especially for children's parties. By colouring the sponge mixture you can create a variety of decorations under the icing to surprise your guests when the cake is cut. Here are just a few of my favourite 'surprise inside' cakes, which are relevant to the projects in this book.

When using food colouring, always check the ingredients and be aware of any allergies in children. While I wouldn't give my children cake containing lots of colouring everyday, I don't mind 'a little treat for a special occasion'! If you are worried about using colouring, just go for natural colours or use the plain and chocolate sponge mixtures (see Cake Recipes).

Cool Camouflage

This really cool effect, perfect for the Paintball Party cake, is created by colouring one third of the cake mixture pale green, one third slightly darker green, and using a chocolate sponge cake mixture for the final third. Carefully place spoonfuls of each mixture randomly into the tin to create patches of the different colours. Bake the sponge in the usual way (see Cake Recipes).

TIP

Add most of the colouring at the butter and sugar creaming stage to avoid overmixing once the flour is added to the mixture.

Perfect Peas

For this fun design used in The Princess and the Pea, baked cake is broken up into crumbs and rolled into balls to make the 'peas'. For enough peas to fill an 18cm (7in) deep cake, bake a 300g (10½oz) (each ingredient) green-coloured sponge mix (I use mint green paste food colouring) in a 23cm (9in) or 25cm (10in) tin (pan) (see Cake Recipes). Allow to cool, then break up into crumbs and mix with 30–45ml (2–3 tbsp) of buttercream. Roll into 2cm (¾in) balls and lightly push them into the tins filled with uncooked cake batter. The balls will sink a little, so you won't need to press them in too deeply. Carefully spoon or spread a little leftover batter over the peas and bake in the oven as usual.

Piñata Party

This colourful sweet-filled design would be great for the Big Top Extravaganza, or you could omit the green and plain-coloured sponge layers to add some extra fun to the Superhero Cityscape. Simply bake thin layers of different coloured sponge (see Cake Recipes), allow to cool and trim and level the cakes (see Layering, Filling and Preparation). Use a cutter to cut out 4cm (1½in) wide circles from the three middle layers. Layer the cake as shown, using a layer with no hole for the base of the cake, and trying not to get any filling in the centre of the cake. Before you put the top layer in place, fill the central hole with sweets, then coat the cake as usual.

Chequered Circles

This design is for a 20cm (8in) cake, and works well with 5cm (2in), 10cm (4in), 15cm (6in) and 20cm (8in) cutters and templates. For a 10cm (4in) or 15cm (6in) cake, simply lose the outer ring. It is eye-catching inside any round cake, or you can scale down the design to make the Knights of the Round Table cake look very effective. Bake two layers of red-coloured sponge and two layers of chocolate sponge: I used a 400g (14oz) mix split between two 23cm (9in) round tins for each colour (see Cake Recipes). Once cool, level and trim each layer to the same height. Cut 5cm (2in), 10cm (4in), 15cm (6in) circles from each layer, making sure they are all centred and layer the cake as shown with a small amount of chocolate buttercream or ganache (see Layering, Filling and Preparation). Smear a little filling inside the circular cuts as you go to help the sponge stick together when cut.

Designer Leopard-Print

To carry over the trendy leopard-print design of the Pretty Print Vanity Case to the inside, bake a 200g (7oz) (each ingredient) mix of very light chocolate sponge (using a small sprinkle of cocoa powder) in a 15–20cm (6–8in) tin and a 250g (9oz) chocolate sponge mix in a 18–23cm (7–9in) tin (see Cake Recipes). To make the leopard-print pattern, make tiny lumps with the broken-up pale sponge combined with 30–45ml (2–3 tbsp) of buttercream. Break up the dark sponge, add the buttercream and pack small pieces around the pale pieces of sponge. Push them into the uncooked cake mixture (see Perfect Peas) and bake as usual.

FILLINGS AND COVERINGS

Fillings give moisture and flavour to a cake. Your choice of filling should complement the type or flavour of the sponge: the most versatile are buttercream and ganache, with ganache generally used for chocolate-covered cakes. Use these recipes on cakes at room temperature and don't refrigerate them until they are ready to serve. Fillings can be used to seal and coat cakes, cover gaps, correct imperfections and create a firm, smooth surface for icing.

Buttercream

Makes about 500g (1lb 2oz); enough for an 18–20cm (7–8in) round or square layered cake, or 20–24 cupcakes.

MATERIALS

- 225g (8oz) unsalted or slightly salted butter, softened

- 275g (9¾oz) icing (confectioners') sugar

- 15ml (1 tbsp) water

- 5ml (1 tsp) vanilla extract or alternative flavouring

EQUIPMENT

- Large electric mixer

- Spatula

1 Put the butter and icing sugar in the bowl of a large electric mixer and mix together, starting on a low speed to prevent the mixture from going everywhere.

2 Add the water and vanilla or other flavouring and increase the speed, beating the buttercream really well until it is pale, light and fluffy.

3 Store for up to two weeks in an airtight container in the fridge.

Sugar Syrup

Sugar syrup can be brushed onto sponge to enhance its flavour and make it moist. Use according to its taste or texture – be careful not to use too much or the sponge will become overly sweet and sticky.

Makes enough for a 20cm (8in) layered, round cake (a square cake will need slightly more), 25 fondant fancies or 20–24 cupcakes.

MATERIALS

- 85g (3oz) caster (superfine) sugar

- 80ml (5½ tbsp) water

- 5ml (1 tsp) vanilla extract (optional)

EQUIPMENT

- Saucepan

- Metal spoon

1 Bring the sugar and water to the boil, stirring once or twice. Add the vanilla extract, if using, and leave to cool.

2 Store in an airtight container in the fridge for up to one month.

Lemon or orange flavour Replace the water with freshly squeezed, finely-strained lemon or orange juice. You can also add a little lemon- or orange-flavoured liqueur (to taste) to heighten the citrusy tang.

Ganache

This luxuriously rich, silky smooth filling is made from chocolate and cream. Ganache sets firmer than buttercream at room temperature, so it gives the cake a nice firm surface to ice on, resulting in sharper, cleaner edges and angles. For this reason, I recommend using ganache for all carved/shaped cakes, such as the Big Top Extravaganza. Always use good quality chocolate with at least a 53 per cent cocoa solids content.

Makes about 500g (1lb 2oz); enough for an 18–20cm (7–8in) round or square layer cake, or 20–24 cupcakes.

MATERIALS

- 300g (10½oz) plain (semisweet or bittersweet) chocolate, chopped, or callets

- 200g (7oz) double (heavy) cream

EQUIPMENT

- Saucepan

- Mixing bowl

- Spatula

1 Put the chocolate in a bowl.

2 Bring the cream to the boil in a saucepan then pour over the chocolate. Stir until the chocolate has all melted and is perfectly combined with the cream.

3 Leave to cool and then cover and store in the fridge. It will keep refrigerated for up to one week.

TIP

Ensure that your ganache or buttercream is at room temperature before using it – you may even need to warm it slightly before spreading.

White Chocolate Ganache

White chocolate ganache is a sumptuous filling for heavy sponge cakes (those that have been made with extra flour) and makes an ideal alternative to buttercream. Simply follow the ganache recipe (see Ganache) but use 150g (5½oz) cream to 350g (12oz) white chocolate. If you are making a small batch, melt the white chocolate before mixing it with the hot cream.

BAKING AND COVERING TECHNIQUES

Layering, Filling and Preparation

Preparing your cakes in the right way ready for icing is essential if you want to achieve smooth, neatly shaped professional-looking cakes. Sponge cakes usually consist of two, three or four layers (see Classic Sponge Cake) and are filled and coated with buttercream or ganache before being iced with sugarpaste (rolled fondant).

MATERIALS

- Buttercream or ganache (see Fillings and Coverings) for filling and covering

- Sugar syrup (see Fillings and Coverings) for brushing

- Jam or conserve (preserves), for filling (optional)

EQUIPMENT

- Cake leveller

- Large serrated knife

- Ruler

- Small sharp paring knife (optional)

- Cake board, plus chopping board or large cake board if needed

- Turntable

- Palette knives

- Pastry brush

2 You should have either baked your cake 2.5cm (1in) larger all around than required or baked a larger sponge (see Classic Sponge Cake). Cut around your cake board (this will be the size of your cake), cutting straight down without angling the knife inwards or outwards. For round cakes, use a small sharp paring knife to do this and for square cakes use a large serrated one.

1 Cut the dark-baked crust from the base of your cakes. If you have two sponges of equal depths, use a cake leveller to cut them to the same height. If you have baked one-third of your cake mixture in one tin and two-thirds in the other, cut two layers from the deeper sponge with a large serrated knife or cake leveller to make three layers. Alternatively, cut three layers from a larger square cake: cut a round from two opposite quarters of the square close to the corners for two layers, then a semi-circle from the other two opposite quarters and piece together for the third layer. Your finished cake will be on a 1.25cm (½in) cake board, so the height of your layers together should be about 9cm (3½in) deep.

3 Place your three layers of sponge together to check that they are all even and level, trimming away any sponge if necessary. Place your base cake board on a turntable. If the board is smaller than the turntable, put a chopping board or another large cake board underneath. Use a non-slip mat if necessary.

4 Using a medium-sized palette knife, spread a small amount of buttercream or ganache onto the cake board and stick down your bottom layer of sponge. Brush sugar syrup over the cake – the quantity will depend upon how moist you want your cake to be.

5 Spread an even layer of buttercream or ganache about 3mm (⅛in) thick over the sponge, then a thin layer of jam or conserve, if using any. Repeat this procedure for the next layer. Try not to add too much filling between the layers of sponge, as the cake will sink slightly under the weight of the icing and ridges will appear. Finish by adding the top layer and brushing with more sugar syrup.

6 Cover the sides of the cake in buttercream or ganache, then the top – you only need a very thin and even layer. If the coating becomes 'grainy' as it picks up cake crumbs, place in the fridge for about 15 minutes to set and then add a thin second coat. This undercoat is referred to as a 'crumb coat' and helps to seal the sponge.

7 Refrigerate your prepared cake for 20 minutes–1 hour to firm it up, before attempting to cover it with icing or marzipan.

FILLING AND COVERING QUANTITIES

Size	10cm (4in)	13cm (5in)	15cm (6in)	18cm (7in)	20cm (8in)	23cm (9in)	25cm (10in)	28cm (11in)
Buttercream or ganache	175g (6oz)	250g (9oz)	350g (12oz)	500g (1lb 2oz)	650g (1lb 7oz)	800g (1lb 12oz)	1.1kg (2lb 7oz)	1.25kg (2lb 12oz)

Carving and Sculpting Cakes

Carving and sculpting sponge allows you to create interesting shapes in your designs, such as wonky cakes or cupcake swirls. It is much easier to carve and sculpt cakes when they are very firm or almost frozen, so wrap them in cling film (plastic wrap) and chill them in the fridge or freezer beforehand.

Cut the sponge away little by little to prevent removing too much. Once you have achieved the desired shape, cover the cake with ganache or buttercream, filling in any holes as you go. If the cake becomes crumbly, place it in the fridge for 15 minutes or so, then give it a second coating. Refrigerate until set and firm enough to cover with icing.

Covering with Sugarpaste

Before icing your cake, cover it with a smooth buttercream or ganache layer to conceal any imperfections that would otherwise be visible. You can cover cakes with a second coat of icing if necessary, or cover with a layer of marzipan before you ice it.

ROUND CAKES

MATERIALS

- Sugarpaste (rolled fondant)
- Icing (confectioners') sugar, for dusting (optional)

EQUIPMENT

- Greaseproof (wax) paper or baking (parchment) paper
- Scissors
- Large non-stick rolling pin
- Large non-stick board with non-slip mat (optional)
- Icing and marzipan spacers
- Needle scriber
- Icing smoother
- Small sharp knife

1 Cut a piece of greaseproof/baking paper 7.5cm (3in) larger around than your cake. Place your cake on top.

2 Knead the sugarpaste until soft. Roll it out with a large non-stick rolling pin either onto the board or a work-surface dusted with icing sugar if the paste is sticky. Use the spacers to obtain the correct width – about 4mm (¼in). Lift the sugarpaste up with the rolling pin and turn it a quarter turn before laying it down to roll again. Try to keep it in a round shape to fit over your cake easily. Push out any air bubbles, or use a needle scriber to burst them.

3 With a rolling pin, pick up and lay the sugarpaste over the cake. Use your hands to smooth it around and down the sides. Pull the sugarpaste away from the sides to unpleat the pleats as you go until you reach the base.

4 Go over the top of the cake with a smoother in a circular motion. For the sides, work around the cake in forward circular movements, almost cutting the excess paste at the base. Trim the excess with a sharp knife. Smooth the cake one final time to ensure a perfect finish.

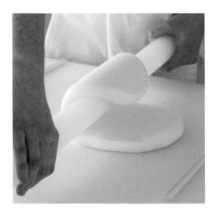

PANELLING METHOD

In order to achieve nice sharp, clean edges, it is sometimes better to ice the cake with 'panels' of sugarpaste or fondant. This basically means covering the different surfaces (top, sides, front, back, etc.) with individual pieces of icing. I have used this method for the Superhero Cityscape, Big Top Extravaganza, Treasured Toy Box and Pretty Print Vanity Case. It will depend on how sticky and soft your icing is as to how ice your cake with panels. If your icing is firm, you can measure the exact size of icing you need and stick it to or wrap it around the cake, trimming just one side. As the icing I use is quite soft, I prefer to trim my sugarpaste to fit the cake as I go, using a clean sharp knife to make each cut.

SQUARE CAKES

Icing a square cake is done in much the same way as a round cake, however you must be careful with the corners to prevent the icing from tearing. Gently cup the icing in your hands around the corners before you start working it down the sides of the cake. Any tears in the icing can be mended with clean soft icing, but do this as soon as possible so that it blends in well.

TIP

Sugarpaste soon dries out and cracks, so you need to work quite quickly. Keep any leftover icing well wrapped in a plastic bag to prevent it from drying out.

CAKE COVERING QUANTITIES

Note: Allow slightly more for square cakes.

Cake size (9cm/3½in deep)	15cm (6in)	18cm (7in)	20cm (8in)	23cm (9in)	25cm (10in)	28cm (11in)
Marzipan/sugarpaste (rolled fondant)	650g (1lb 7oz)	750g (1lb 10oz)	850g (1lb 14oz)	1kg (2lb 4oz)	1.25kg (2lb 12oz)	1.5kg (3lb 5oz)

Securing Ribbon Around Cakes and Boards

To secure ribbon around the base of a cake, first measure how long the ribbon needs to be by wrapping it around the cake so that it overlaps by about 1cm (⅜in). Trim to length with a sharp pair of scissors. Attach double-sided tape to either end of the ribbon on the same side. Stick one end directly in place onto the icing, then wrap the ribbon around the cake and stick the other end, overlapping, onto the first end. For square cakes, put the double-sided tape around each corner as well as a small piece in the centre of each side.

For professional results, attach double-faced satin ribbon around the edge of the cake board in a matching or complementary colour. Use 1.5cm (⅝in) wide ribbon and secure at intervals around the board with double-sided tape.

Icing Cake Boards

For a clean, professional finish to your cake, cover the base cake board with icing.

1 Moisten the board with some water. Roll out the sugarpaste (rolled fondant) to 4mm (⅛in) thick, ideally using icing or marzipan spacers. Place the board either on a turntable or bring it towards the edge of the work surface. Pick the icing up on the rolling pin and lay it over the cake board so that it is hanging down over it.

2 Use your icing smoother in a downward motion to cut a smooth edge around the board. Cut away any excess icing. Finish by smoothing the top using circular movements to achieve a flat and perfectly smooth surface for your cake to sit on. Leave to dry overnight.

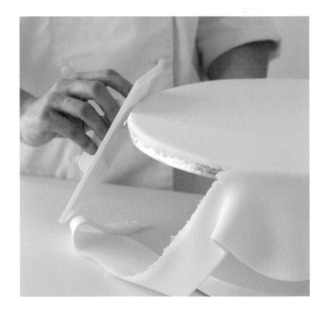

CAKE BOARD COVERING QUANTITIES

Cake board size	23cm (9in)	25cm (10in)	28cm (11in)	30cm (12in)	33cm (13in)	35.5cm (14in)
Sugarpaste (rolled fondant)	600g (1lb 5oz)	650g (1lb 7oz)	725g (1lb 9½oz)	850g (1lb 14oz)	1kg (2lb 4oz)	1.2kg (2lb 10½oz)

Assembling Tiered Cakes

Stacking cakes to create a series of tiers is a fairly simple process, but you need to follow the correct procedure to ensure that the structure of the cake is firm and reliable. I advise using hollow plastic dowels because they are sturdy and easy to cut to the correct height. Thinner plastic dowels or even large strong straws are suitable for smaller cakes. See the chart below as a guide to the number of dowels you will need.

MATERIALS

- Iced cake board (see Icing Cake Boards)
- Stiff royal icing (see Royal Icing)

EQUIPMENT

- Cake top marking template
- Needle scriber or marking tool
- Hollow plastic dowels
- Edible pen
- Large serrated knife
- Spare cake board
- Spirit level
- Icing smoothers

1 Use the cake top marking template to find the centre of your base cake.

2 Using a needle scriber or marking tool, mark the cake where the dowels should go. These need to be positioned well inside the diameter of the cake to be stacked on top. Push a dowel into the cake where it has been marked. Using an edible pen, mark the dowel where it meets the top of the cake.

3 Remove the dowel and cut it at the mark with a large serrated knife. Cut the other dowels to the same height and insert into the cake. Place a cake board on top of the dowels and check that they are equal in height by using a spirit level on the board.

4 Stick your base cake onto the centre of the iced cake board with stiff royal icing. Use your smoothers to move it into position if necessary. Leave the icing to set for a few minutes before stacking on the next tier. Repeat to attach a third tier if needed.

DOWEL QUANTITIES

Cake size	15cm (6in)	20cm (8in)	25cm (10in)
No. of dowels	3–4	3–4	4–5

Mini Cakes

Mini cakes are small round or square cakes that are cut from a large square cake then layered, filled and iced in a similar way as full-size cakes. The number and size of cakes you want will determine the size of the large cake, but it is best to opt for one slightly larger than your requirements to allow for wastage. I make my square mini cakes 5cm (2in), so to make nine you will need an 18cm (7in) square cake. Refer to the charts in the Cake Recipes section, but use only two-thirds of the ingredient quantities, as mini cakes are shallower. Bake all the mixture in one tin (pan) rather than dividing it between two as you would for a larger cake.

MATERIALS

- Large square baked classic sponge cake (see Cake Recipes)

- Sugar syrup (see Fillings and Coverings)

- Buttercream or ganache (see Fillings and Coverings)

- Sugarpaste (rolled fondant)

EQUIPMENT

- Cake leveller

- Circle cutter or serrated knife

- Pastry brush

- Cake card (optional)

- Palette knife

- Large non-stick rolling pin

- Large non-stick board with non-slip mat

- Metal ruler

- Large sharp knife

- Large circle cutter or small sharp knife

- Two icing smoothers

MINIATURE ROUND CAKES

1 Slice your large square cake horizontally into two even layers using a cake leveller. Cut small individual rounds with a cutter.

TIP

You will find it easier to work with the sponge if it's very cold, as it will be much firmer.

2 Brush the pieces of sponge with sugar syrup and sandwich together with either buttercream (plus jam if desired) or ganache if using a chocolate-flavoured cake. It's easier if you stick the bottom piece of cake to a cake card the same size and shape as your mini cake using buttercream or ganache, but not essential. Working quickly, pick up each cake and cover the sides evenly with buttercream or ganache. Finish by covering the top and then place the cakes in the fridge for at least 20 minutes to firm up.

3 Roll out a piece of sugarpaste 38cm (15in) square and 5mm (¼in) thick with a large non-stick rolling pin on a large non-stick board set over a non-slip mat. Cut nine small squares and lay one over each cake. If you are a beginner, prepare half the cakes at a time, keeping the other squares under cling film (plastic wrap) to prevent them from drying out.

4 Use your hands to work the icing down around the sides of the cake and trim away the excess with a large circle cutter.

5 Use two icing smoothers on either side of the cake going forwards and backwards and turning the cake as you go to create a perfectly smooth result. Leave the icing to dry, ideally overnight, before decorating the cakes.

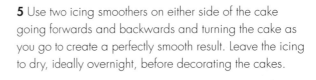

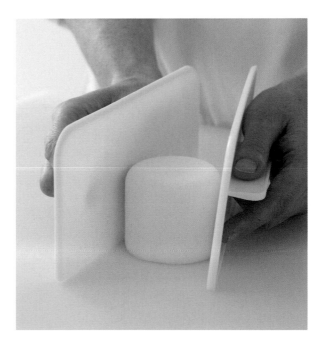

Miniature Square Cakes

Square mini cakes are created in a similar way to the round ones, so follow the instructions for Miniature Round Cakes. Cut out squares of cake using a serrated knife and use a sharp knife to cut away the excess icing around the sides of the cake. Use smoothers on opposite sides to press and smooth the icing around the four sides. Finish the cakes by using smoothers on opposite sides to press and smooth the icing around the four sides.

Baking Cupcakes

To bake the cupcakes in this book follow the Classic Sponge Cake recipe used for the full-size cakes. To make a batch of 10–12 cupcakes, use the quantities given for a 13cm (5in) round or 10cm (4in) square cake.

To bake the mixture, place cupcake cases (liners) in tartlet tins (pans) or muffin trays (pans) and fill them two-thirds to three-quarters full. Bake in a preheated oven at 180°C/350°F/Gas Mark 4 for about 20 minutes, until the cakes are springy to touch.

I prefer to use plain foil cupcake cases, available in a range of colours, because the foil keeps the cakes fresh and there is no pattern to draw attention away from the decoration on the cakes. But they also come in plain or patterned paper, and you can use decorative cases for plainer cupcakes.

Covering Cupcakes with Sugarpaste

Sugarpaste (rolled fondant)-covered cupcakes are quick and easy to make. Simply use a cutter to cut out a circle of sugarpaste and place it inside the cupcake top. Use cupcakes that have a nice even, slightly domed shape and trim them if necessary.

1 Using a palette knife, spread a thin layer of flavoured buttercream or ganache over the cakes so that it forms a perfectly rounded and smooth surface for the icing to sit on.

2 Roll out some sugarpaste and, using a circle cutter, cut out circles that are very slightly bigger than the cupcake top. I would suggest cutting out nine at a time and covering any circles that you are not using with cling film (plastic wrap). Cover the cupcakes one at a time, using the palm of your hand to drape the icing out to the edges to completely cover the tops of the cupcakes.

Buttercream-Topped Cupcakes

The quickest and simplest way to ice a cupcake is to top it with buttercream. The cupcakes themselves don't need to be perfectly shaped, as the buttercream topping will hide any imperfections.

1 Before you prepare or ice the cupcakes, make sure they are completely cool. Brush the tops with extra sugar syrup if you think they might be a little dry, or if you want them to be really moist (see Fillings and Coverings).

2 You can also 'inject' jams or conserves (preserves) into your sponge before you top them with buttercream. Simply fill a squeezy bottle with a narrow-pointed nozzle with the jam or conserve, carefully insert it into the cupcakes and squeeze.

3 To pipe your cupcakes, fit a large disposable plastic piping (pastry) bag with a large plain or star-shaped tube (tip), fill with buttercream (see Fillings and Coverings) and pipe a kiss (peak) or swirl onto the top – it will take a little practise to get each cake looking perfect.

4 Alternatively, simply use a palette knife to spread the buttercream on evenly to create a neat domed top. Make sure your icing is soft when you use it – you may need to re-beat it or even warm it slightly if the room temperature is fairly cold.

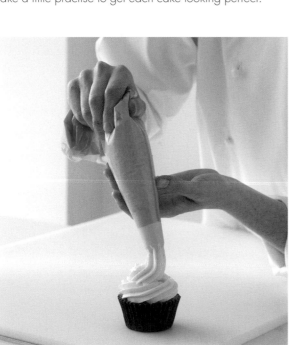

Baking Cookies

Cookies also give you plenty of creative scope, as you can cut all manner of shapes from the dough and decorate them in many different ways to suit every occasion. They offer an ideal opportunity to involve children and have some fun with their preparation. For added convenience, cookies can be made well in advance of an event.

SHELF LIFE

The cookie dough can be made a few days ahead or stored in the freezer until ready to use. The baked cookies will keep for up to one month.

MATERIALS

- 250g (9oz) unsalted butter
- 250g (9oz) caster (superfine) sugar
- 1–2 medium eggs
- 5ml (1 tsp) vanilla extract
- 500g (1lb 2oz) plain (all-purpose) flour, plus extra for dusting

EQUIPMENT

- Large electric mixer
- Spatula
- Deep tray or plastic container
- Rolling pin
- Cookie cutters or templates
- Sharp knife (if using templates)
- Baking trays (sheets) lined with greaseproof (wax) paper or baking (parchment) paper

1 In a large electric mixer, beat the butter and sugar together until creamy and quite fluffy.

2 Add the eggs and vanilla extract and mix until they are well combined.

3 Sift the flour, add to the bowl of the mixer and mix until all the ingredients just come together. You may need to do this in two stages – do not overmix.

TIP

Don't add too much flour when you are rolling out your cookies or they will become too dry.

4 Tip the dough into a container lined with cling film (plastic wrap) and press down firmly. Cover with cling film and refrigerate for at least 30 minutes.

5 On a work surface lightly dusted with flour, roll out the cookie dough to about 4mm (⅛in) thick. Sprinkle a little extra flour on top of the dough as you roll to prevent it from sticking to the rolling pin.

6 Cut out your shapes either with cutters or using templates and a sharp knife. Place on baking trays lined with greaseproof (wax) or baking paper and return to the fridge to rest for at least 30 minutes. Meanwhile, preheat your oven to 180°C/350°F/Gas Mark 4.

7 Bake the cookies for about 10 minutes, depending on their size, or until they are golden brown. Leave them to cool completely before storing them in an airtight container until you are ready to decorate them.

ADDITIONAL FLAVOURINGS

Chocolate Substitute 50g (1¾oz) flour with cocoa powder (unsweetened cocoa).
Citrus Omit the vanilla and add the finely grated zest of one lemon or orange.
Almond Replace the vanilla with 5ml (1 tsp) almond extract.

Cookie Pops

Cookie pops are so fun to create and children will love them! Simply bake your cookies following the instructions above, inserting the sticks into the dough before you cut out the shapes. You can't cut through where the stick goes into the dough so use a knife to carefully cut around that area.

DECORATING TECHNIQUES

Royal Icing

Royal icing is such a versatile medium, as it can be used for icing cakes and cookies, intricately piping decorations or for simply attaching and sticking. Learning to work with royal icing is a one of the most important skills to acquire in cake decorating.

 For best results, use royal icing while it is as fresh as possible, however it will keep for up to five days when stored an airtight container. If it is not used immediately, re-beat the mixture back to its correct consistency before use.

MATERIALS

- 2 medium egg whites or 15g (½oz) dried egg albumen powder mixed with 75ml (5 tbsp) water

- 500g (1lb 2oz) icing (confectioners') sugar

EQUIPMENT

- Large electric mixer

- Sieve (strainer)

- Spatula

Soft-Peak Royal Icing

You may need to add a tiny amount of water to your royal icing to soften it slightly so that it pipes easily. When you pull up the icing, peaks should form and softly and slowly collapse down, rather than staying upright.

1 If using dried egg powder, soak it in the water for at least 30 minutes in advance, but ideally overnight in the fridge.

2 Sift the icing sugar into the bowl of a large electric mixer and add the egg whites or strained reconstituted egg mixture.

3 Mix together on a low speed for about 3–4 minutes until the icing has reached a stiff-peak consistency, which is what you need for sticking on decorations and gluing cakes together.

4 Store the icing in an airtight container covered with a damp, clean cloth to prevent it from drying out.

Run-Out Icing

Royal icing is thinned down with water to 'flood' cookies (see Royal-Iced Cookies). Test for the desired consistency by lifting your spoon and letting the icing drip back into the bowl – it should remain on the surface for five seconds before disappearing. If it is too runny it will run over the outlines and sides of the cookies; if it is too stiff it won't spread very well.

Making a Piping Bag

1 Cut two equal triangles from a large square of greaseproof (wax) paper or baking (parchment) paper. As a guide, for small piping (pastry) bags cut from a 15–20cm (6–8in) square and for large bags cut from a 30–35.5cm (12–14in) square.

2 If you are right-handed, keep the centre point towards you with the longest side farthest away and curl the right-hand corner inwards. Bring the point to meet the centre point. Adjust your hold so the two points are together between right thumb and index finger.

3 With your left hand, curl the left point inwards, bringing it across the front and around to the back of the other two points in the centre of the cone. Adjust your grip so that you are holding the three points together with both thumbs and index fingers. Tighten the cone by gently rubbing your thumb and index fingers forwards and backwards until you have a sharp tip at the end of the bag.

4 Carefully fold the back of the bag (where all the points meet) inwards and press hard along the fold. Repeat to secure.

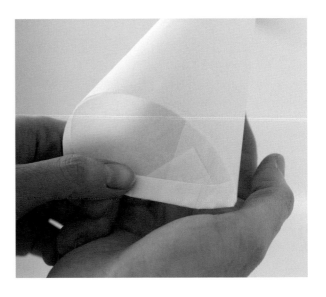

TIP

Make lots of piping bags at a time and put them aside for a decorating session.

Piping with Royal Icing

Use soft-peak royal icing (see Royal Icing) for basic piping work. The size of the tube (tip) you use will depend on the job at hand and how competent you are.

Fill the piping (pastry) bag until it is no more than one-third full. Fold the top over, away from the join, until you have a tight and well-sealed bag. The correct way to hold the piping bag is important. Use your index finger to guide the bag. You can also use your other hand to guide you if it's easier.

To pipe dots squeeze the icing out gently until you have the dot that's the size you want. Stop squeezing then lift the bag. If there is a peak in the icing, use a damp brush to flatten it down.

To pipe teardrops once you have squeezed out the dot, pull the tube through the dot, then release the pressure and lift the bag. To pipe elongated teardrops and swirls, squeeze out a ball of icing and drag the icing round to one side to form a swirl or scroll. Increase the pressure and amount of icing you squeeze out for longer, larger shapes. Keeping close to the surface you are piping on is known as 'scratch piping'.

To pipes lines touch the tube down, then lift the bag up in a smooth movement, squeezing gently. Decrease the pressure and touch it back down to the point where you want the line to finish. Try not to drag the icing along, or it will become uneven. Use a template or a cookie outline as a guide where possible.

To 'drop in' icing 'drop' a different coloured, runny icing into the flooding icing while it is still wet. This gives a slightly different and more blended effect, rather than just piping directly onto the top of the dry cookie.

Royal-Iced Cookies

This is my preferred method of icing cookies – I love the taste of the crisp white icing against the softer texture of the cookie underneath. Use a squeezable plastic bottle with a small tube instead of piping bags if you are icing a large quantity of cookies.

MATERIALS
- Soft-peak royal icing (see Royal Icing)

EQUIPMENT
- Small and large paper piping (pastry) bags (see Making a Piping Bag)
- Piping tubes (tips) nos. 1 and 1.5

1 Place the no. 1.5 tube in a small paper piping bag and fill with some soft-peak royal icing. Pipe an outline around the edge of each cookie, or the area that you wish to ice.

2 Thin down some more royal icing with water until 'flooding' consistency (see Run-Out Icing) and place in a large paper piping bag fitted with a no. 1 tube. Use to flood inside the outlines on the cookies with icing. For larger cookies, you can snip off the end of the bag instead of using a tube. If the area you need to flood is relatively large, work around the edges of the piped outline and then inwards to the centre to ensure an even covering.

3 Once dry, pipe over any details that are required and stick on decorations as desired.

Working with Flower Paste

Flower (petal/gum) paste can be rolled out very thinly, making it fantastic for creating delicate icing decorations for cakes and cookies, such as flowers, frills and bows. Some brands of sugarpaste (rolled fondant) icing are already quite stiff, so you may not always need to use flower paste.

Before using the paste, knead it thoroughly by continuously pulling it apart with your fingers. It often helps to let the paste dry a little once you have cut the shape before attaching it to the cake. Flower paste dries out quickly, so make sure you store any leftover paste immediately in a plastic bag.

Modelling Paste and CMC

Modelling paste is similar to sugarpaste (rolled fondant), only stiffer in consistency, which allows you to mould larger, more robust shapes and decorations, such as the bears in Teddy Bears' Picnic and the toys in the Treasured Toy Chest. It isn't as strong and doesn't dry out as quickly as flower (petal/gum) paste. You can buy modelling paste ready-made, but it's cost-effective and very easy to make your own using CMC (sodium carboxymethyl cellulose), which comes in the form of a powder that you knead into sugarpaste. As a guide, use about 1 tablespoon (15ml) per 300g (10½oz) icing.

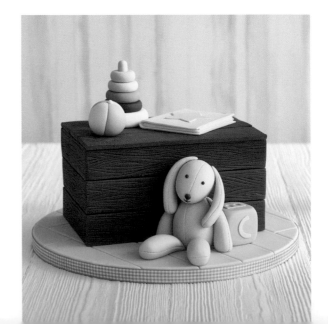

Colouring Icing

Three kinds of food colouring are used to colour icing: paste, liquid and, less commonly, powder. I prefer to use paste for colouring because it prevents the icing from becoming wet and sticky. Add small amounts with a cocktail stick (toothpick) and larger amounts with a knife and then knead it into the icing. Always add colouring gradually, keeping some extra white icing to hand in case you add too much colour. Liquid food colour is good for colouring royal icing, but be careful not to add too much too soon. Be aware that the colour of icing can change as it dries – some colours tend to fade while others darken.

TIP

It is best to colour more icing than you need, to allow for mishaps. Any leftovers can be stored in an airtight bag in a sealed container.

Making Edible Glue

Edible glue is used for sticking paste items together and onto the cakes. It is easy to make; simply add 40ml (1½fl oz) of cooled boiled water to 0.8ml (1/16tsp) of CMC. Mix it to dissolve for 10–20 minutes. To thicken the glue, add more CMC; to thin the mixture, add more water.

Edible Icing Sheets

Edible icing sheets are a great way to get a decorative surface design onto your cake fast! Edible images and photos have been around for a while and they are basically photos or images printed onto edible paper with edible ink. More recently, printed patterns have become available – but even better than that, you can design your own! For the Superhero Cityscape I have just created a simple dot pattern, however the options are endless. If you don't have the skills or resources to design and print your own, there are many downloadable printables available online (you will need to check the copyright first) or you can email me and I can send them to you (see Suppliers). You can also send your files to a decorating supplier who will print what you need.

Templates

All templates are shown at 50% size and will need to be enlarged by 200%.
Download printable templates at http://ideas.stitchcraftcreate.co.uk/patterns

BABY BUTTONS AND BUNTING & CUTE ELEPHANT COOKIES

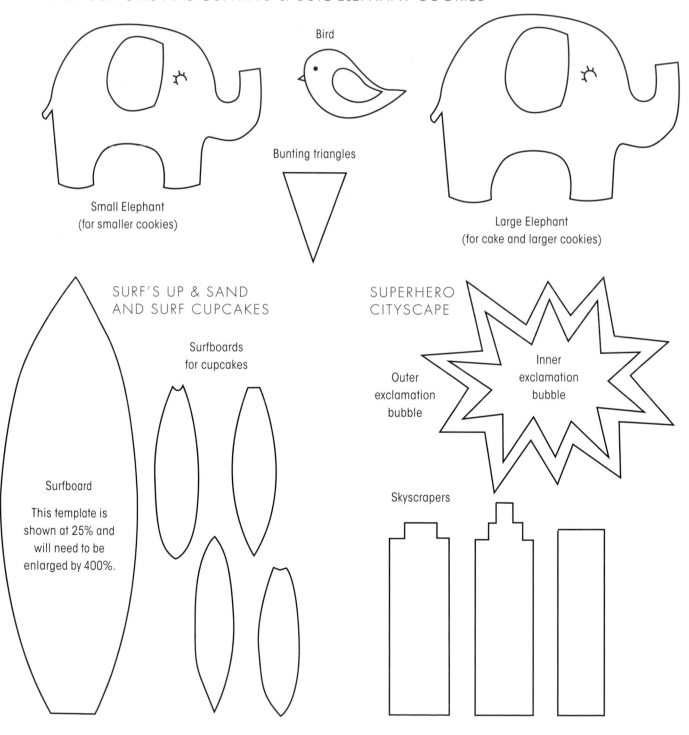

Bird

Bunting triangles

Small Elephant
(for smaller cookies)

Large Elephant
(for cake and larger cookies)

SURF'S UP & SAND AND SURF CUPCAKES

Surfboards
for cupcakes

Surfboard

This template is
shown at 25% and
will need to be
enlarged by 400%.

SUPERHERO CITYSCAPE

Outer
exclamation
bubble

Inner
exclamation
bubble

Skyscrapers

THE PRINCESS AND THE PEA

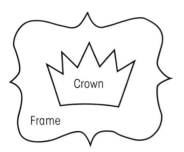

KNIGHTS OF THE ROUND TABLE

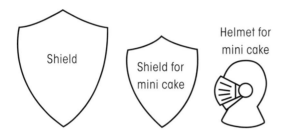

GARDEN GANG COOKIES

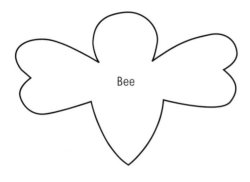

BIG TOP EXTRAVAGANZA

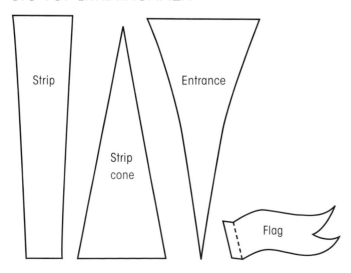

MAGNIFICENT MASK COOKIES

Mask shapes

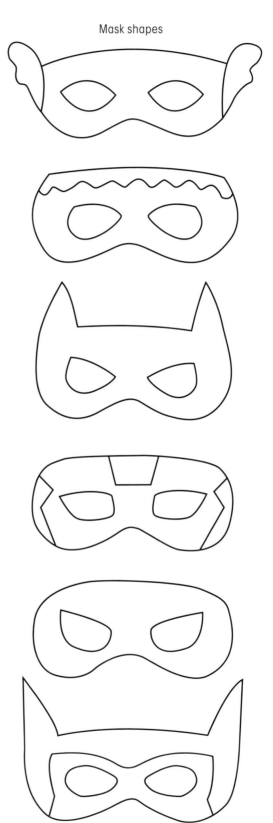

Suppliers

UK

Zoe Clark Cakes
www.zoeclarkcakes.com

Purple Cupcakes
www.purplecupcakes.co.uk
Tel: 0115 969 9800

Stitch Craft Create
www.stitchcraftcreate.co.uk
Tel: 0844 880 5852

Squires Kitchen
www.squires-shop.com
Tel: 0845 61 71 810

The Cake Decorating Company
www.thecakedecoratingcompany.co.uk
Tel: 0115 969 9800

US

Global Sugar Art
www.globalsugarart.com
Tel: 1-518-561-3039

Australia

Cakes Around Town
www.cakesaroundtown.com.au
Tel: 07 3160 8728

Couture Cakes
www.couturecakes.com.au
Tel: 02 8764 3668

Acknowledgments

First of all I'd like to thank my Photographer, Mark, Art Designer, Vic, and Editor, Beth, for all their hard work and help with this book.

As always, I'd like to thank my amazing and supportive family and staff, without whom I'd never be able to do the things I do!

Finally a special thank you to Jackson, Maya, Melody and Phoebe for being such angels and great models!

About the Author

Zoe Clark is one of London's leading cake designers, and her work regularly appears throughout the world in bestselling bridal and sugarcraft magazines. Her cake designs have also featured on television and in films, and she has previously produced six books for D&C showcasing her unique style. Zoe opened The Cake Parlour in South West London in November 2010, where as well as offering a bespoke cake and confectionery design service for every occasion she also runs cake-decorating classes for aspiring cake decorators from all over the country and beyond. Zoe travels the world teaching and you can find her tutorials online.

www.zoeclarkcakes.com

Index

A DAVID & CHARLES BOOK
© F&W Media International, Ltd 2014

David & Charles is an imprint of F&W Media International, Ltd
Brunel House, Forde Close, Newton Abbot, TQ12 4PU, UK

F&W Media International, Ltd is a subsidiary of F+W Media, Inc
10151 Carver Road, Suite #200, Blue Ash, OH 45242, USA

Text and Designs © Zoe Clark 2014
Layout and Photography © F&W Media International, Ltd 2014

First published in the UK and USA in 2014

Zoe Clark has asserted her right to be identified as author of this work in
accordance with the Copyright, Designs and Patents Act, 1988.

A catalogue record for this book is available from the British Library.

ISBN-13: 978-1-4463-0426-6 paperback
ISBN-10: 1-4463-0426-4 paperback

Printed in China by RR Donnelley for:
F&W Media International, Ltd
Brunel House, Forde Close, Newton Abbot, TQ12 4PU, UK

10 9 8 7 6 5 4 3 2 1

Acquisitions Editor: Ame Verso
Editor: Emma Gardner
Project Editor: Beth Dymond
Senior Designer: Victoria Marks
Photographer: Mark Scott
Production Manager: Beverley Richardson

F+W Media publishes high quality books on a wide range of subjects.
For more great book ideas visit: www.stitchcraftcreate.co.uk